HUSSEIN OF JORDAN: My "War" with Israel

HUSSEIN
OF JORDAN:
MY "WAR" WITH ISRAEL
As told to and with
additional material by
VICK VANCE and
PIERRE LAUER

translated by June P. Wilson
and Walter B. Michaels

WILLIAM MORROW

AND COMPANY, INC.

NEW YORK / 1969

DS
127.9
J6
H83

58016

*Printed in the United States of America
by Cornwall Press, Inc., New York*

Design by Winston Potter

Library of Congress Catalog Card Number 78–79099

Contents

5

Preface

The story of the Israeli part in the "lightning war" of 1967 has already been told many times.

What happened on the Arab side has remained vague, not to say ignored.

It is therefore of prime importance to understand King Hussein's position, since he may be considered the spokesman for the Arab camp.

Why?

Because Jordan, more than any other Arab country, is geographically, humanly, politically and economically involved in the fate of its neighbor Israel.

Because Jordan, in June 1967, found itself forced to enter into the conflict even though it knew it had nothing to gain from it.

Because, during this conflict, the Jordanians were the only members of the Arab camp who respected and accepted their obligations.

Because, now that this new drama is over, the badly mauled Jordanians have been the first to direct their energies toward a constructive search for a solution to the Palestinian problem.

Since King Hussein was the only Arab leader to participate personally in the battles of June '67, his evidence is of primary importance.

And so what follows is a report of what we heard and saw, thanks to the willingness to accept reality and the regard for the truth that characterize the head of the Jordanian state. At no point is there a question of judgment, criticism, accusation or self-justification. King Hussein has been content to trace the causes leading up to the events of June 1967, the events themselves and their consequences, without shrugging off his own responsibilities.

We have done our utmost to represent faithfully our conversations with King Hussein.

Vick Vance and Pierre Lauer

HUSSEIN OF JORDAN: My "War" with Israel

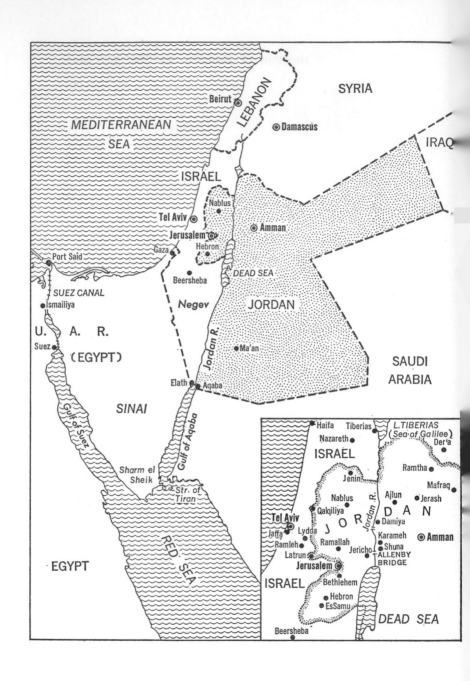

Chapter 1
The Inevitable Conflict

"Everything we tried to do
was sabotaged . . ."

King Hussein speaks:

From the day the United Nations troops were withdrawn from Gaza, I foresaw the consequences of this decision. To me it was obvious: war with Israel was inevitable.

In the first place, the Israelis were doing their best to create the same situation that preceded the conflict of 1956. They were giving a lot of publicity to the raids of the Arab commandos which they cleverly exploited with a carefully orchestrated propaganda designed to win them the sympathy of the entire world.

In the second place, the Arab position was not particularly satisfactory. To cite a few examples chosen among many, you need only recall the Israeli aggression in Es Samu, Jordan, in November 1966, and the deteriorating situation along the line of the Syrian armistice which came to a climax with the air action of April 7, 1967, provoked by a raid of Israeli planes over Syria. (Result of this new aggression: six Syrian Migs brought down in one hour.)

And don't forget the statements of Eshkol and other Israeli leaders who threatened to attack and even occupy Syrian positions if Damascus continued to protect the commandos of the P.L.O. [Palestine Liberation Organization]. And finally, Damascus's answer when, having summoned the ambassadors of the great powers, it informed them of Tel Aviv's aggressive intentions by noting the massive concentration of Israeli forces on its borders.

This series of incidents led inescapably to Nasser's decision to arrange his troops in defensive positions in the Sinai Peninsula. In fact, the day after the air engagement over Syria on April 7, 1967, the United Arab Republic and Syria revived their bilateral defense pact. The signing of this separate defense treaty had resulted from the impasse that bogged down the last summit conference of the Arab countries at Casablanca in September 1965. This impasse had left the United Arab Command paralyzed.

To get a better idea of the seriousness of this lack of a unified Arab command on the one hand, and on the other —a corollary of this deficiency—the separate signing of a military pact between two Arab states in disregard of the common defense pact, it is important to remember the situation of the Arab armed forces at this time.

From January 1964 to September 1965, the Arab leaders met three times: in Cairo, Alexandria and Casablanca. The first of these summit conferences was held, at Nasser's request, in the Egyptian capital on January 17, 1964.

I wish to point out that 18 months before, on July 2, 1962, I had made public a report entitled: "Jordan, the Palestinian Question and Arab Relations" (better known to the public as the "White Book"). This report set forth the Jordanian point of view on the vital need to unify the Arab world.

I have repeated over and over again: unity in the Arab world is essential if we are ever to get what is our due. Today more than ever, I am convinced that this unity is imperative. That is why Nasser's initiative in calling a summit conference in 1964 seemed to me entirely right.

On the agenda of this first summit conference, top priority was given to an examination of the available means of preventing Israel from diverting the waters of the Jordan River to its own benefit. Our problem, obviously, was to protect Arab interests. But how?

The first obstacle, and a big one, was that we had to rule out any kind of military solution. At this period, the use of force against Israel was out of the question in view of the political and military situation in most of the Arab countries.

Therefore we decided that, until we were ready to use arms, our best solution was to divert certain tributaries of the Jordan ourselves in order to reduce the damage that would result from the Israeli irrigation projects.

But this could only be a palliative. At the same time, it became clear to us that we had to set up an organization whose goal would be the creation of a real Arab armed force coordinating all our respective military means against an eventual Israeli threat. This organization was named the "United Arab Command." We placed at its head the Egyptian General Ali Amer.

If the problem of the Jordan was the principal subject at this summit meeting, the Palestinian question remained extremely important. The Arab League suggested the formation of the Palestine Liberation Organization and designated Ahmed Shukairy as its leader.*

---

* Ahmed Shukairy had been a lawyer in Jerusalem up to the partition of Palestine in 1948. He then turned against Haj Amin El Husseini, the aged mufti of Jerusalem in whose entourage he had been, in order to launch his career as a politician, a career in which he made himself a "millionaire refugee."

As assistant secretary of the Arab League, he became a Syrian in order

In any event, this latest initiative was officially accepted so as to thwart Israel's pretense that the Palestinian problem didn't exist. As a matter of fact, the Israeli point of view implies that, as a result of the events of 1948, the Palestinians have lost their national identity since they now had the option of assuming Jordanian nationality. However, contrary to Tel Aviv's assertions, the problem is not so easily solved, for the Palestinians have never renounced their claims as expressed in the United Nations resolution. And so this affair is not buried, as Israel would have us believe. Far from it!

More than any other Arab country, the Palestinian question concerns us Jordanians directly. As a result, we welcomed the principle behind the Palestine Liberation Organization, and were ready to give it our unreserved support, with only one condition: the P.L.O. had to cooperate with Jordan without a trace of friction.

Indeed, the welcome we extended to the Palestinian refugees in Jordan was unique in the entire Arab world.

We had made it possible for a third of the Palestinian population to become one people with the Jordanians, from the west bank of the Jordan to the east. In Jordan, the Palestinian could, without a single restriction and sim-

---

to represent Damascus in Cairo. But immediately after the Suez campaign of 1956, he exchanged this for Saudi Arabian nationality so that he could represent that country at the United Nations. It was then that he threatened in a speech to "throw the Jews into the sea" and thereby set much of the world's moderate opinion against the Arabs. He was dismissed when King Faisal came to power and it was Nasser who found him the "job" that would make him world famous: head of the Palestine Liberation Organization and charged with the task of creating a Palestinian army to be placed under the authority of the United Arab Command.

He made himself an element of discord as an instigator of internal battles within the Arab world, and harmed only the Arabs by his blundering and excessive statements against the Israelis.

ply by asking, take on Jordanian citizenship, with rights identical to those of any other Jordanian citizen in every domain: civil, political, military, etc.

This was hardly the case in the other Arab countries. They were content to open their doors to the Palestinians only as refugees, with no privileges except that of living in camps until things should take care of themselves.

We wanted at all costs to preserve the integration we had brought off with no little difficulty, and that is why we demanded that the P.L.O. cooperate without friction and refrain from sowing discord between us, whatever the pretext.*

Looked at as a whole, the military situation in the Arab countries was poor. Admittedly, our means were of unequal value and quite incapable of facing any kind of military adventure. It was this reason basically that drove us to put together an organization that could combine and coordinate our common defense potential. A unified Arab command was all the more essential as any talk of equality between Arab and Israeli forces became laughable.

I need only point out that the Israelis had brought their internal stability and military power to the highest degree, whereas the Arab multitudes were stretched over a vast area, racked with the most delicate political and economic

* Concerning the creation of the P.L.O., it is interesting to remember the opinions of Jordanian politicians and foreign observers who considered this organization advocated by the Arab League "a political movement created by Socialist Egypt to foment trouble in royalist Jordan and to keep the Palestinians under its thumb." H. E. Wasfi al Tall, who was Prime Minister of Jordan until April 1967, expressed it thus: "Shukairy was an instrument of Egypt which had as an ulterior motive the destruction of our troublesome monarchy. According to most foreign political observers, our success was a source of embarrassment to Cairo and Damascus Socialism."

problems. The most obvious in 1964 was the instability of several Arab states.

In this context, try to imagine an invasion of Jordan by Israel. Can you conceive realistically of effective intervention—that means in the shortest possible time—by Algerian or Moroccan forces!

At the time of the first summit conference in Cairo, there were those who advocated the encirclement of Israel, so as to discourage Tel Aviv from continuing its diversion of the waters of the Jordan. Under no circumstances was this argument justified.

In the first place, each of the Arab armies was equipped with different matériel, some coming from the West, some from the East. It was the same with our training methods and technical backgrounds. They were different.

In addition, and this was no doubt our worst military handicap, the tactical theories of the various Arab armies were based on different teaching by foreign instructors of varying origins. As a result, each Arab country fashioned a defense strategy that conformed to its own criteria which, if it worked, ran counter to the strategy of one of its allies.

Under these conditions, any concerted action was irrevocably doomed.

Lastly, in 1964, some of the Arab countries were unable to achieve a military collaboration because they were totally immobilized by their internal politics, the result of incompetent leaders poorly qualified to direct a nation's affairs.

After considering all these factors, we arrived at the following conclusion: faced with a unified Israel, the Arabs had to build their own unity at all costs. And so, the first act of the Cairo summit meeting was the establishment of the United Arab Command to head our collective forces of defense.

But the time factor had to be taken into account. Israel was a bomb which threatened to explode at any moment, since the problem it represented was insoluble. Hence the urgent necessity to bring about Arab military unity.

Originally, Israel was a religious invention that drained people from all over the world onto Arab soil. But as time passed, the objective took on far greater importance than was officially indicated at the beginning. This was clearly demonstrated by the constant expansion of Israel's geographic frontiers. With each change, the menace grew. You need only compare the Israel created by the U.N. in 1947 with the Israel of 1948 and, later on, the new Israel of 1956 with that of 1967. This proves the extent of the Israeli threat to the Arab world.

By the time the second summit conference was called in Alexandria from September 5 to 12, 1964, the organization and aims of the United Arab Command had already run into a host of difficulties. Then at the third summit conference held in Casablanca a year later, on September 19, 1965, it ground to a halt.

At this final meeting, we carefully assessed the cooperative actions we had taken, both political and military, since our first meeting in Cairo, 20 months earlier.

On the military side, in 1965, the United Arab Command was beginning to make some progress. But it needed additional financial resources if it was to arrive at its goal of reestablishing a balance between Arab and Israeli forces in the three years allotted. To mean anything, this balance had to give the Arabs a slight superiority in order to make the Israelis stop and think, and to discourage them from planning any kind of military adventure. To achieve this goal, we must respect the three-year minimum, and furnish the United Arab Command with the financial resources for such needs as a larger air force in Jordan. We Jordanians were incapable of providing this luxury, for all that it was indispensable to the Arab cause. Without it an effective modern army is out of the question. But an air force is not just a matter of buying planes. You need a whole technical complex—air bases, radar—let alone the time to train pilots and ground personnel.

In spite of the high stakes involved, the United Arab Command's request for additional funds was rejected by the majority of the Arab leaders, who claimed they could not possibly afford it. In desperation, we asked General Ali Amer to cut his budget. For our part, we agreed to do everything in our power to solve the Arab problems whose repercussions, financial and otherwise, were hampering the United Arab Command.

For example, I need only cite the war raging in Yemen between the United Arab Republic and Saudi Arabia, and the Iraqi's attempt to reestablish order in the face of the Kurds' rebellion in the north. There is no point in listing the whole series of problems which arose out of internal crises in certain countries due to a lack of political maturity or because of a lust for power.

If all these various difficulties had been solved as they occurred—or, in other words, if each part had really wanted to solve its problems for the sake of the whole—the Arab world would have been able to move ahead and realize its program for common action. Even if we had not completely achieved our goal by the end of the three years, we would still have acquired experience and cohesion on a perfectly respectable level.

It was now becoming more and more urgent! Israel was actively developing its military potential, and, thanks to its scientific capacities, was producing very advanced armaments, particularly in the area of nuclear weapons and an army trained to use them. Once again, the balance of power was upset. And weren't we aware of it!

Consequently, we owed it to ourselves to bring off our program in the agreed time in order to create a favorable climate wherein we could attract the world's attention to the Palestinian problem and thus find a solution. By the same stroke, if we did our work well, the Arab world would have acquired a position it had never held up to then.

To the many difficulties undermining the work of the United Arab Command must be added the unfortunate activities of the Palestine Liberation Organization.

At the time of the first summit conference in 1964, the heads of state and the U.A.C. warned the members of the conference against furnishing Israel with the slightest pretext for starting a premature war. It was stated on several occasions—in instructions we received in Amman—that the commando raids had to cease during this period that was so essential to the achievement of our common defense and to the avoidance of a situation like that of 1956. In other words, we didn't want to give Israel the opportunity to start fighting before we were ready.

Actually, the commandos' activities began to attract attention *after* the first Arab summit conference and not before. If the Palestinians had wanted to serve their cause effectively and force the attention of the Arabs in particular and the world in general to their problem, logically their leaders should have acted before and not after the Cairo meeting where we had just tried, for the first time, to do something positive and concrete to solve their problem.

Be that as it may, everything we undertook was sabotaged by the commando actions and their inopportune timing.

We were so conscious of the danger they represented that we issued a new warning to the Palestine Liberation Organization during the third and final summit conference in Casablanca.

Personally, from the very beginning and up to the conflict of June 1967, I was suspicious of this period of relative peace. It seemed to me abnormal. It was too easy for Israel to bring it to an end, using "acts of terrorism" as a pretext, with negligible harm to Tel Aviv.

The consequences were not slow in coming. Soon after the summit meeting in Casablanca, Jordan plunged into a serious crisis with the Palestine Liberation Organization and the essential unity of the Arab world began to tremble at its foundations. There was a crack, then complete disintegration. The scaffolding supporting Arab solidarity came crashing down.

From 1965 on, the P.L.O. became a state within the Arab states and did as it liked. Its machinations, added to all the other factors I have just mentioned, virtually put the United Arab Command out of commission. It could no longer function under these conditions.

On the subject of the P.L.O.'s activities, Wasfi al Tall, the Jordanian Prime Minister during this period, ex-

plained why and how the terrorists of the P.L.O. flouted the authority of the Arab leaders:

Before the first Arab summit meeting, the commandos were an independent movement (since the P.L.O. did not yet exist) given to very limited action. Their activities moved into high gear after the Cairo summit which to many Arabs was a cruel deception. And for good reason! Everyone had kept insisting: if the Israelis divert the waters of the Jordan, the Arabs will immediately take up arms to oppose it.

But no such thing happened! When the Israelis moved to divert the Jordan, everybody turned to Nasser. It was he who then called together the first Arab summit meeting.

When the Palestinian terrorists learned the results of the Cairo conference, they immediately figured it to be a maneuver of Nasser's to keep the Arabs at bay and under his control. Disappointed, they began to act on their own and with much greater zeal, even though the Cairo reunion was the parent of the P.L.O. and its supporting army under the control of Ahmed Shukairy.

After the third summit meeting, Egypt resumed her quarrel with Saudi Arabia over Yemen, and with Jordan over the P.L.O. From then on there was no possibility of a fourth summit meeting.

In 1966, it was I (I was at that time President of the Jordanian Council) who closed the offices of the P.L.O. in Jordan. They had begun to practice subversion on a grand scale. They were trying to divide the populations of the east and west banks of the Jordan. They were taking into their ranks people who belonged to what we considered illegal political parties, such as the Baathists [under Syria's socialist-military rule, the Baathists are the only official party], Communists and leftist nationalists. Actually, their goal was to replace Jordan's monarchy with some other political authority.

Immediately, our problems with Egypt and Syria began to worsen.

The fact is that the P.L.O. was a political movement having no connection whatever with the commandos. It had an army based in Egypt, in Gaza, Syria and even in Iraq. Here, in Jordan, we had not authorized such an army's formation. Even more, we had refused to let them send us troops. The Palestinians living in Jordan had become Jordanian citizens without restrictions of any kind, and under no conditions did we wish to offer up the Hashemite kingdom to the divisions which existed elsewhere.

Therein lay one of the reasons for our misunderstandings with Cairo and Damascus.

Moreover, even though the P.L.O. was based in Syria, it attacked Israel by crossing Jordan. And so, the Israelis responded by attacking Jordan and Syria together. The threat to both countries became almost permanent. The threat to Syria pushed Nasser into adopting measures which in the end led us all into war. It was a vicious and infernal circle!

The closing of the P.L.O. offices in Jordan by the government of Wasfi al Tall was followed up by a speech delivered by King Hussein on June 14, 1966, before the École Normale in Ajlun. It sounded the death knell for the Palestinian organization in the Hashemite kingdom. In his speech, the King also made a declaration of faith in his unshakable position on the many great questions facing the Arab nations. He said, in substance:

The Palestinian problem no longer concerned only the Palestinians but the entire Arab world from the moment the Arab armies penetrated Palestinian soil in 1948.

The Palestinian cause found its voice in 1964 with the first of the summit conferences.

The first meeting in Cairo placed the problem above the differences and antagonisms that affected the Arab coalition.

All commando activities other than those decided upon by the Arab leaders at that meeting were useless if not actually harmful.

We wanted the P.L.O. to be a mirror reflecting the unity of Arab Palestine—a catalyst for its energies, an organization that would harness all the Palestinians' vital forces.

Under the influence of communism, the P.L.O. was no longer a movement of liberation. It had gone off its course and become a melting pot for all the discordant and displaced elements in the Arab world.

We believe the unity of the two banks of the Jordan to be the key to greater Arab unity. Those who work to separate the two banks are sapping Jordanian and Arab strength.

To take theatrical positions makes no sense.

Separatism is the road to foreign intervention in our affairs. Marxist ideology will take advantage of this to penetrate our country. Russia has coveted our land since the days of the tsars.

We don't believe for a moment that the U.S.S.R. or Communist China is helping us simply out of kindness.

To attack the countries of Islam who oppose communism is to attack Islam's interests.

First and foremost, we hold that we are Arabs and that Arab nationalism makes sense only within its religious framework, meaning Islam.

We believe in Arab unity, which is the goal of the younger generations in all the Arab countries.

More than anything else, we insist on the necessity of Arab cooperation because our border with Israel is the longest.

Our enemy's strength is based on a scientific turn of mind that knows exactly what it wants. Our weakness is not caused by Western imperialism but by our own ignorance.

Our job is twofold: we must strengthen our army and develop our country.

We need revolutions in many areas: in increased political freedom and means of communications, a demographic revolution and a revolution in what we know and believe, a revolution in our ideas and hopes for humanity.

In conclusion, the Hashemite sovereign appealed to future students of the École Normale of Ajlun:

All this can be realized through education. You are the teachers of tomorrow. Our future lies in your hands.

Chapter 2
The Israeli Attack
of November 1966

"Dark days loomed in the
Middle East."

The King continues:

By the end of the third summit conference in September 1965, it was clear that Arab unity had been undermined. The same held true for the United Arab Command, which for all practical purposes had ceased to exist. Finally the unfortunate maneuvers of the P.L.O. and the activities of the commandos had managed needlessly to compromise an already shaky peace which the Arab world had needed desperately in order to arrive at a solution to the Palestinian question.

On November 13, 1966—under the pretext of "reprisals against the terrorist activities of the P.L.O."—Israeli forces attacked Es Samu, a Jordanian village of 4,000 inhabitants, all of them Palestinian refugees whom the Israelis accused of harboring terrorists from Syria.

Es Samu sits on a high point dominating the road from Hebron on the west bank of the Jordan, about five kilometers north of the Israeli border.

The Israeli attack began at 5:30 in the morning with a burst of artillery that covered the penetration of 4,000 Israeli soldiers in jeeps, armored cars and five Patton tanks. They surrounded the Jordanian village, which was defended by the local police; and, while demolition teams dynamited 46 houses and the hospital, the tanks moved up to the police station and leveled it. The minaret of the village mosque was hit.

At 6:15, some 20 Jordanian trucks and a few armored cars rushed from Hebron to relieve Es Samu. But, since the village overlooked the road, the Israeli lookout was able to sound the alarm. Our rescue column fell into the ambush the enemy had had time to prepare. Our planes intervened. But as soon as they arrived our four Hawker Hunters were set upon by several Israeli Mirages. They were caught off guard and one Hawker Hunter went down.

At 9:30, the Israelis departed across the border. This "punitive" operation had lasted four hours. The cost to us: 21 dead and 37 wounded, not to mention heavy losses in matériel.

The affair was brought before the United Nations. The Security Council condemned Israel by a large majority: 14 votes and one abstention—that of New Zealand. Even the Americans joined with the Russians, British and French. The United States delegate, Arthur Goldberg, described the Israeli raid as "inexcusable."

Following the "Es Samu affair," some of my Arab allies, instead of going after Israel, turned against me! I had hardly expected such a reaction and I must admit I was flabbergasted and confused.

Their reaction was a result of my refusal, in accordance with the directives of the United Arab Command, to accept the idea that Shukairy's men were to launch their raids on Israel exclusively from Jordan. It was too easy!

Why didn't they use other Arab borders as their launching pads—Egypt, Syria or Lebanon, for example?

In any event, on November 23, 1966, 10 days after the Es Samu incident, Wasfi al Tall, my Prime Minister, held a press conference to bring matters into proper focus and answer the accusations against me. Wasfi al Tall pointed out:

1. That the attack on Es Samu should have served as a test for the United Arab Command since this large-scale operation took place along the armistice line. This was the line of demarcation drawn up in Cairo at the signing of the Arab common-defense pact. This meant in effect that any Israeli aggression against a point on this line had to be considered as an act of aggression against all the Arab countries.

2. When the Israelis moved against Es Samu, Jordan needed air support. This was the responsibility of the United Arab Republic, according to the defense plan of the United Arab Command which had assigned coverage of the air space south of Jerusalem to the Egyptian air force.

3. We would tolerate no isolated commando infiltration without our knowledge because we intended to abide by the resolutions adopted by common consent at the three Arab summit conferences. Those resolutions stipulated, and were firm on this point, that all commando actions against Israel had to be submitted to review by the United Arab Command before they were carried out, since it alone had the authority to judge if the proposed operation was a "coordinated action" as defined by the Arab states. As my Prime Minister pointed out, the U.A.C. was under instructions particularly to avoid all risk of giving Israel an excuse

to open hostilities for which the Arabs were not prepared.

After the aggression against Es Samu to which we had reacted vigorously and alone, things got worse not only between Jordan and Israel but also between Jordan and our Arab allies, except for Saudi Arabia. From then on, I became the target of the Syrians, the Egyptians and especially the Palestine Liberation Organization.

There is no use dwelling on the verbal assaults which were directed at me. I learned by way of the international press and "The Arab Voice," the Cairo radio and that of Damascus, that "before liberating Tel Aviv, we must liberate Amman!"

In Cairo, they went so far as to say that "if an army is incapable of defending its borders, like Jordan, we must arm and train the people in the border villages." Yet our conduct at Es Samu was proof enough that we had not let the Israelis go scot-free. And we had been alone! As for the border population, it was in fact already trained and armed, but what could it have done against a concerted attack by superior forces?

All that remains to be said is that the Israeli raid against Es Samu set off an even more serious chain of events. Dark days loomed in the Middle East. Nor were they slow in coming. The virulence of our new adversaries was bearing fruit.

The Council of the Arab League was called in extraordinary session in Cairo. Theoretically, the aim of this meeting was to examine what became known as "the Es Samu affair." However, no one was fooled. It was simply open warfare inspired by those who prided themselves on being "revolutionaries" against the Hashemite and Saudi Arabian monarchies which they labeled "reactionary." Whatever they said, I always preferred to call my school that of the "evolutionaries."

Among the participants at this conference, Ahmed Shukairy—although he was invited only as an observer—was far and away the most violent against me. As the head of the P.L.O. had it, "the kingdom of Jordan must become the Palestinian republic," and "the first thing that must be done is to station an army of the P.L.O. in Jordan," of which this gentleman was to be the "general." The official mission of this force would be to defend the Jordanian borders against any new Israeli aggression. And what with? With an army formed between now and tomorrow, which was simply childish and out of the question.

Cairo's aggressiveness made inroads on Jordan where Baathists, Communists and left-wing nationalists demonstrated against the regime. (This was only the twelfth time since I came to the throne in 1952 that I had had to cope with plots hatched beyond our borders!) The demonstrations spread, taking on the aspect of an insurrection. Its center was the west bank of the Jordan. In Hebron, Nablus, Ramallah and Jenin, agitators aroused the Palestinian refugees. My government had no choice: a state of emergency was declared. The army moved in to reestablish order even though it must also be ready to face new Israeli attacks. Meanwhile tension mounted, thanks to the virulent campaign waged against the Hashemite kingdom by the P.L.O. through the facilities of "The Arab Voice" in Cairo.

On Friday, November 25, 1966, the P.L.O. broadcast two statements that carried the tone of an ultimatum. The first demanded "the resignation before noon tomorrow, Saturday, November 26, 1966, of all ministers of Palestinian origin in the Jordanian cabinet." The second statement called on "all members of the police and Jordanian security forces to refrain from opposing demonstrations against the regime." Instead, the Cairo voice declared, "the police should join the demonstrators in order to help press their demands."

Finally, Ahmed Shukairy addressed a speech to all the Arab countries inviting the faithful to pray for "the martyrs of the Jordanian army and the Jordanian people."

On this same Friday, violent skirmishes broke out in Jerusalem between the demonstrators and the forces of law and order. These demonstrations grew to such a size that the next day, my government—which had remained at its post despite the P.L.O.'s exhortations to resign—declared Jerusalem in a state of siege.

But the reestablishment of order is one thing, the stability of a country's institutions another. That is why I decided to prove that my detractors were wrong: I changed neither my Parliament nor my government, though both were in fact 50 per cent ex-Palestinians.

I repeat, in spite of the "Shukairy order," there was not one defection, not one resignation. What is more, when I opened the new session of Parliament, there was not a trace of hostility; quite the reverse, I was cheered and applauded.

Still, it was 10 days before calm was restored and life got back to normal. And, it must be admitted, the most serious consequence of those events was the breakdown of Arab unity. Its effect would be felt inside Jordan as well as outside.

Inside, where the Palestinian question had found itself questionable champions after the "Es Samu affair," everything was far from resolved. Quite the contrary.

Outside, world approval which we needed so much kept its distance.

Moreover, the pace of events was quickening, bringing proof of what I had warned.

Chapter 3
The Deterioration

"On May 22, Nasser announced the
closing of the Strait of Tiran . . ."

During the five months following the "Es Samu affair," the situation between Arabs and Israelis grew progressively worse until, on April 7, 1967, a battle broke out pitting Israeli Mirages against Syrian Migs. This engagement over Syria was followed by a massive concentration of Israeli forces along the Syrian border.

From this moment on, events moved inexorably toward war.

The Arabs reacted immediately. In line with the Egyptian-Syrian defense agreement, Marshal Abdel Hakim Amer, Vice-President of the United Arab Republic and head of its armed forces, issued his first order of the day: "A state of maximum alert is declared as of 2:30 P.M., May 15, 1967, over all Egyptian territory."

As it happened, on May 15, Israel was celebrating its nineteenth anniversary with a military parade in Jerusalem which the foreign diplomatic corps had refrained from attending because of the Holy City's questionable status.

In Egypt, Nasser announced that he had ordered troops sent toward Sinai, under the pretext of relieving the Syrians from Israeli pressure on their border.

At almost the same moment, we learned from the Egyp-

tian press and radio that General Mahmoud Fawzi, the
Egyptian Chief of Staff, had sent a note to the Indian
General Indrajat Rikie, Commander of the United Nations
Emergency Force based on Sinai's demilitarized zone. This
note demanded the withdrawal of the U.N. forces from the
line of demarcation where they had been stationed since
February 26, 1957—following the second Israeli-Arab confrontation of November 1956—and their regrouping in the
region of Gaza.

The troop movements effected by Nasser for the occupation of Sinai seemed intended as a deterrent. Did they have
the desired effect on Tel Aviv? The fact remains that the
17th of May passed without incident. According to Arab—
and they say even Russian—intelligence, this was the date
originally fixed by Israel to launch its attack against Syria.

On May 18, U Thant, Secretary-General of the United
Nations, without consulting the Security Council, agreed
to evacuate the U.N. forces from the demilitarized zone at
Gaza.

This surprising move on the part of the U.N. Secretary-
General was unprecedented. I was now convinced that a
military confrontation with Israel was inevitable. I immediately called a meeting, which lasted four hours, with
Saad Jumaa, my new Prime Minister, the cabinet and the
high-ranking officers on the General Staff of the Jordanian
Armed Forces, which we placed on alert.

At 4 P.M. on May 19, the U.N. forces began their withdrawal into Egypt. A few hours later, the two Palestinian
regiments in Gaza completed the occupation of the 73 observation posts abandoned by the U.N. forces. On the
Israeli side, preparations for the attack moved into high

gear. On May 20, the Egyptian forces took up position at Sharm El Sheik overlooking the Strait of Tiran.

And at this point—on the 21st of May—in the midst of the escalation between Tel Aviv and Cairo-Damascus, the Syrians could think of nothing more suitable than to send us a car which exploded on our border at Ramtha. It had been meant to explode in the center of Amman. Result: 14 Jordanians killed.

This compelled us to sever diplomatic relations with Damascus.

The incident filled Jordan with unease. In such delicate circumstances, we no longer knew who was less trustworthy: Israel, or our Arab allies! An added handicap on the eve of war.

On May 22, the day after our incident with the Syrians, Nasser left on a tour of inspection in Sinai. It was then that he announced the closing of the Strait of Tiran, to become effective at midnight on May 23.

With the closing of the Gulf of Aqaba, Nasser appeared to expect an Israeli reaction. He reinforced his positions in Sinai and mobilized reservists. All the same, I don't think the Egyptian President wanted it to come to actual war. I even suspect he didn't really believe war would break out. In my view, it was inescapable.

The U.S.S.R. foresaw the obvious complications and went so far as to issue a warning to Israel. And in Paris, General de Gaulle advised Abba Eban, Israel's Foreign Minister who was on his way to President Johnson in Washington: "Above all, don't be the first to shoot." He repeated this several times.

In any event, I was convinced that it was no longer possible to pull back or to put out the smoldering fire. Israel was already beating the drums and preparing its psychological campaign to win over world opinion all the while brandishing its sword.

On the other hand, if the Arab world was threatened, this threat included us Jordanians too, and for two important reasons:

My first reason for taking precautions was dictated by one simple fact. It was true that, up to then, Israel had directly threatened only Syria and Egypt. Couldn't Jordan have stayed out of the conflict, as I have often been asked since?

No.

To begin with, in June, we were all bound by the Pan-Arab defense pact signed in Cairo during the first summit conference. This pact had never been revoked, even after the disappointments of the last conference before the conflict.

But even without this agreement, should war break out, it would involve us all. We knew this from experience:

In 1956, the Israelis had opened hostilities against Egypt under the pretext that they were being harassed by terrorists coming from Jordan.

In 1966, the Israelis complained this time that the terrorists operated out of Syria, and so it was we in Jordan who took the brunt of the "punitive expedition" against Es Samu.

The conclusion was obvious: the differences among the Arabs were significant only to the Arab camp. To the Israelis, we were all alike. We were all Arabs!

My second reason was a moral one. Even though serious disturbances had broken out in Jordan in November 1966 following Es Samu—disturbances clearly provoked by my allies to embarrass me—I could under no pretext behave toward them as I had accused them of behaving toward me. So there was never a question of my breaking away from the Arab camp and standing aside from a conflict that threatened us all. Especially since I thought our unity was essential to our mutual security and Arab survival. That is why I tried—disregarding the persistent hostility of some of our allies toward Jordan—to restore the ties that were supposed to bind us.

To do this, I proposed in an official communiqué to open our borders to Saudi Arabian and Iraqi troops so that we would be reinforced in the defense of our 650-kilometer border with Israel, and thereby discourage the inevitable Zionist offensive, or at least limit the damage. I was well aware that Tel Aviv's principal objective was to occupy the west bank of the Jordan where our presence was a permanent danger so long as the Palestinian question was unresolved.

Since no Arab country was capable of meeting the Israeli threat alone, it seemed essential that we coordinate everyone's capabilities before the battle was joined. And so I decided to communicate with Nasser.

Overlooking the fact that for a year our relations could not have been worse, I proposed through the intermediary of the United Arab Republic's embassy in Amman that we have a discussion to determine what might be necessary to relieve the threat that imperiled the Arab world.

Now more than ever, I believed that personal differences had to give way to national interests.

Chapter 4
The Meeting with Nasser,
May 30, 1967

On May 30, 1967, King Hussein, at his own request, met with President Nasser in Cairo. Zeid Rifai, Chief of Protocol at the Royal Palace in Amman and private secretary to the King, remained at his sovereign's side during the conflict of June 1967 and the events that preceded it.

Zeid Rifai came originally from Safed on the shores of the Lake Tiberias (Sea of Galilee) in Palestine, and was born into a family of diplomats. His father, Samir Rifai, was Prime Minister of Jordan. His uncle, Abdel Moneim Rifai, was Ambassador to Cairo and since June 1967 Minister of Foreign Affairs. He is married to the daughter of the current Prime Minister, Bahjat al-Talhouny.

Zeid Rifai was the man closest to the King of Jordan. Because of his responsibilities, he lived in the shadow of the sovereign and became his confidant. Obviously, his testimony is of first importance.

Zeid Rifai was educated at the British Victoria College in Egypt and at Harvard University in the United States, where courses in Islamic theology turned him into a passionate advocate of Arab interests and a spearhead for nationalist Jordanian youth. He was dynamic and ambitious, and a brilliant political future was predicted for him.

He was adroit with weapons, like everyone in King Hussein's entourage. Of medium height, solid, light-skinned, with hair streaked almost blond like his mustache, he was an elegant man who hid, under his relaxed appearance and circumspect smile, a keen intelligence and a will of iron.

Here is Zeid Rifai's version of the surprising "reconciliation" between Hussein and Nasser which seemed inexplicable to foreign observers at that time:

When Nasser closed the Strait of Tiran, the King realized that war was inevitable. As with the withdrawal of the U.N. Emergency Force, Jordan was neither consulted nor warned. It was from the Cairo radio that we picked up these two fairly important bits of information, as did the rest of the Arab world and the Soviet allies of the U.A.R., a fact which Moscow complained of bitterly.

This is how it all happened:

On the morning of Monday, May 22, I was at my desk in the palace as usual when I received a telephone call from Radio-Amman informing me that Radio-Cairo had just announced the closing of the Gulf of Aqaba.

At 1 P.M., the King arrived at his office. He called me in. He had already heard the news and was deeply troubled.

"This is very serious," he said. "I think war is inevitable now."

But all we did was take note of the event. Nothing more.

It is true that, for a year, Jordan had been on the outs with the Arab world and had had to put up with a constant flow of jibes and slurs from the Egyptians. So we refused to get in touch with Cairo to hear their explanation. We were tired of always being the one to take the first step. Since the withdrawal of the U.N. forces from Gaza, the King—who was very unhappy with the turn of events—had made several advances in Cairo's direction. We wanted to revive the machinery of Arab unity which, faced with this danger, was more important than ever. All these advances had been sidetracked and lost in Cairo's silence.

For several days, nothing happened. Once the first moment of shock had passed, life went back to normal. Tensions relaxed. We observed the diplomatic skirmishes set off by the "Gulf affair."

Meanwhile, 48 hours after the closing of the Gulf, we asked for reinforcements through our diplomatic channels in Saudi Arabia and Iraq. A simple precautionary measure in the face of an increasingly explosive situation, and also completely in accordance with the principle of the common-defense pact signed by the Arab countries in Cairo in 1964. Reinforcements were not forthcoming. Or, to be more exact, the Saudi Arabian troops would arrive when everything was over. The Iraqis gave us a flat "No!"

On May 28, there was a new step in the process of escalation: In Cairo, at a radio press conference before 300 journalists, President Nasser said: "If the Israelis want war, then I say '*Ahlan Wa Sahlan*' ('Go to it, we are ready!')." Or, in so many words: "Sirs, you be the first to shoot!"

With my ear to the radio I kept on my desk, I followed Nasser's press conference from beginning to end. I fully understood then that His Majesty's fears were justified. With this, war had to follow.

The King too heard the Egyptian President and immediately decided to send General Amer Khammash, Chief of Staff of the Jordanian Army, to Cairo. General Khammash's mission was to get in touch with the United Arab Command which, from the time of the first summit conference, had had its headquarters in Egypt. He was to study with its leaders their plans for opposing an eventual Israeli attack.*

When he returned from Cairo, General Khammash informed the King that the United Arab Command was finished, thanks to the differences between Egypt and the other Arab countries. These quarrels had brought the Command's activities to a complete halt.

General Khammash was also told that the Command had no role in present plans. Egypt was conducting the affair bilaterally with Syria.

On that same day, the Parliament in Cairo granted Nasser full powers, and declared a state of emergency at all airports in the U.A.R.

Faced with the situation's obvious deterioration, the King decided to make a last try at a reconciliation with Egypt. He summoned the ambassador of the U.A.R. in Amman, Osman Nouri, and told him of his wish to meet with Nasser as soon as possible. The King stressed the importance of such a meeting to coordinate our defenses in the face of the Israeli threat.

The desire to meet with Nasser may well seem strange in view of the insults broadcast by Radio-Cairo over the past year. But on no account had we any right or reason

---

* General Khammash was originally from Salt, between Karameh and Shuna on the east bank of the Jordan. A married man with three children, he was 42 years old and had devoted 27 years to a brilliant career first in the air force, then in the Jordanian Army. Dark-skinned, short but solid, Amer Khammash was loyal and dependable. The King relied on him in all military matters. He was a specialist in the logistics of modern warfare. Besides, he was looked upon favorably by Westerners. After the debacle of June 1967, it was he whom Hussein chose to reorganize the armed forces. General Khammash had the military know-how to make decisions and then act upon them.

to evade an affair in which the Arab world was unques-
tionably going to be involved.

Cairo's response arrived late during the night of May
29. It was Saad Jumaa, the Jordanian Prime Minister, who
immediately informed the King by telephone: Nasser welcomed the King's initiative.

On Tuesday morning, May 30, with the sun barely risen,
the King chartered a Caravelle from ALIA. [This is the
Jordanian air transport company, named after the King's
oldest daughter.] At 7 A.M., he took off from the airport
at Amman. There was a full crew on board. But as usual,
the King took over the controls. King Hussein is too active
a man to let himself be driven, whether in a car or a plane.
He has said himself: "It relaxes me to pilot a plane, and it
gives me much pleasure besides."

An interesting detail: The King was wearing a khaki
combat uniform and a cap with the emblem of his crown
and his rank of marshal. He was armed with an American
357 Magnum with six automatic barrels lodged in a canvas
holster fixed to his belt over the left hip. Since the start of
the crisis, the King had been in uniform like the rest of us.

No bodyguards, no secret service personnel, not one
policeman accompanied him. One of his typical bold ges-
tures.

Before the take-off, His Majesty said:

"I'll probably be back for lunch," which in Jordan
means about 1:30 P.M.

The discussion with Nasser lasted longer than he had
anticipated. The King did not return at the stated hour,
but lunched with Nasser in the palace at Koubbeh, at one
time the residence of King Farouk.

Because the departure of the King for Egypt was kept a

secret, here in the palace at Amman, the entire staff had its ear to Radio-Cairo. We had developed the habit during the past 15 days. Since Cairo had adopted its independent course, it was our only means of keeping up with developments.

In my office next door to the King's, I too stayed glued to my transistor.

At 3:30 P.M., Radio-Cairo interrupted a program for a "flash bulletin": "King Hussein and President Nasser are about to sign a treaty of mutual defense. The ceremony will be broadcast."

We all breathed a sigh of relief.

Chapter 5

The Reconciliation of the Enemy Brothers:

THE SIGNING OF THE MILITARY PACT BETWEEN JORDAN AND EGYPT

"My trip to Cairo caused
a lot of talk."

The King speaks:

On Tuesday, May 30, I left Amman for Cairo, escorted to our borders by planes of the Jordanian air force. I departed in such a hurry that the formalities for the transfer of power—any of my absences made this act essential—took place between my car and the plane, on the tarmac. I signed the official documents during this few meters' walk, and my younger brother, Prince Mohammed, took the oath of office.

I had only a few people with me on this trip: Saad Jumaa, my Prime Minister, General Amer Khammash, Army Chief of Staff, Saleh Kurdi, head of the air force, and an air force captain as aide-de-camp.

Our destination was the Egyptian military airport at Almaza. We had decided our mission should be kept a secret. I stayed at the controls of the Caravelle until we began the descent toward Cairo, then gave my place over to the pilot.

I was tense and excited by the turn of affairs. And the results of my mission caused me great anxiety.

Nasser met me at the Almaza air base, accompanied by his Prime Minister, M. Mahmoud Soudki Souleiman, and his four vice-presidents. General Ali Amer, head of the United Arab Command, was there too.

We limited our greeting to a handshake. My initiative seemed to have pleased him although I detected a certain reserve.

Gradually, however, the confrontation became more cordial. Some Egyptian photographers stood at a distance, waiting for permission to take pictures.

"Do you think it's all right?" Nasser asked me. "Or would you prefer that we kept the visit secret?"

"It doesn't matter. They'll find out, sooner or later."

Then in a joking tone, Nasser noted: "Well, I see that you are armed and in uniform!"

"It means nothing," I said. "We've been dressing this way for more than a week."

It was true. Ever since the closing of the Strait of Tiran, I had been inspecting troops up to the level of companies. This would go on right up to the moment hostilities broke out in June.

Nasser was wearing a business suit. With a note of irony, he answered back:

"Since your visit is a secret, what would happen if we arrested you?"

"The possibility never crossed my mind," I said with a smile.

And I cut short this awkward conversation before it took an unfortunate turn.

In the black Cadillac that took us from Almaza to the palace at Koubbeh, I outlined to Nasser the reasons for my coming and the necessity for coordinating our efforts in the light of our present situation.

It was absolutely essential that the United Arab Command rise from its ashes.

The King's narration was interrupted and he was asked: Did you believe at that time that if Egypt and Syria joined forces, they could defeat Israel?

No, not alone.

Even with a military potential as large as that of the United Arab Republic?

There was certainly a slight superiority in matériel. But even so I doubted that they could defeat Israel. The Israelis had been getting ready for a long time. Their real strength lay in the superior organization, administration and training of their troops. In the most optimistic light, I could see a slight advantage. But I never believed in a total victory. On the other hand, I never thought that Israel could win so easily.

But to get back to my trip to Cairo. As soon as we reached the palace at Koubbeh, Nasser and I went into a small drawing room on the first floor where we immediately tackled the problems before us. We went through them all: our mutual relations, the situation that faced us, the necessity for serious and effective coordination, the measures we had to take.

Then Marshal Abdel Hakim Amer, U.A.R. Vice-President, head of the Egyptian Armed Forces and at this period Nasser's "dauphin," joined us, followed by Saad Jumaa, my Prime Minister, and other Egyptian and Jordanian leaders. I suggested that we utilize the United Arab Command.

"I have no objection," Nasser answered. "But it will be hard to use the U.A.C. because of the agreement I signed with Syria . . . And then there are all the other problems of the Arab world of which you are well aware.

"I have another solution," he added. "We can draw up a pact between our two countries right here and now."

At my request, he sent someone to find the file containing the bilateral defense pact between Egypt and Syria which had bound the two nations together since April. I was so anxious to come to some kind of agreement that I merely skimmed the text and said to Nasser:

"Give me another copy. Put in Jordan instead of Syria and the matter will be settled."

In an atmosphere of growing relaxation and cordiality, Nasser agreed, and a little later, I signed.

I then explained my problems with Ahmed Shukairy. At the conclusion of our conversation, Nasser sent for the President of the Palestine Liberation Organization. He had been summoned from Gaza specially for the occasion. Shukairy came in, bareheaded, tieless, in a long-sleeved shirt and khaki pants, looking particularly unkempt. No sooner was he in the room than he rushed up to me with hand outstretched. We took our places around the table to sign the defense treaty, the Egyptian delegation on one side, the Jordanians on the other. At that moment, without being invited, Shukairy sat down with the Jordanians. After the signing, he launched into a long tirade, stating that he considered me the leader of the Palestinians, that he hoped that what had been agreed to in the treaty would really come to pass, and I don't know what else . . . then he added:

"I hope to visit Jordan in the near future . . ." which

Nasser interrupted with: "You are not going to Jordan in the near future. You are leaving with His Majesty this very day!"

Then turning toward me, he added, laughing:

"You may take Shukairy with you. If he gives you any trouble, throw him into one of your towers and rid me of the problem!"

Everybody burst out laughing. The fact is that Shukairy and his radio had long been broadcasting a host of stories about Jordanian prisons where, it appears, we threw free and innocent men into towers and made them submit to nameless practices. Which, I might mention, is completely untrue.

Not in the least put out, Shukairy telephoned his house and asked to have a suitcase delivered immediately to the airport at Almaza.

But to get back to the serious business of this trip: the Egyptian General Abdel Moneim Riad, Assistant Chief of Staff of the United Arab Command, joined us a little later in the conference room, together with some other officers. Nasser appointed him to direct the operation from Amman. But before going to Amman, Riad was to head an Egyptian delegation leaving Cairo for Baghdad and Damascus that very day. His mission was to explain the situation to the Iraqi and Syrians and hasten preparations for our common defense against the eventual Israeli offensive.

We had already called President Abdel Rahman Aref in Baghdad. Nasser talked first, announcing to him the signing of the Jordan-Egypt defense pact. Then I took the phone and Aref told me that he was pleased with the new turn of events and was ready to help us to the best of his abilities.

The official ceremony of the signing of our mutual-defense pact took place after lunch. I was now in a hurry to get back to Amman. On our way to the airport, Nasser suggested we visit the new headquarters of his armed forces in Heliopolis, which we did, but very quickly. The atmosphere was more and more relaxed and friendly. Marshal Abdel Hakim Amer repeated several times, in the name of the Egyptian army: "We are glad that you are once again in the family picture. It strengthens our confidence."

My trip to Cairo caused a lot of talk.

The fact is that my trip was forced on me by the obvious superiority of the forces opposing us. All my meetings with my officers were based on the certainty that hostilities were imminent. It was unfortunate, but once again we were forced to act on this assumption. It was already too late to prepare ourselves as we would have liked. From now on, we would have to improvise according to Israeli maneuvers. Unlike Israel, the Arabs were without a unified operational plan. We Jordanians tried to pull our weight as a diversion, thus minimizing the damage when war came. We had no real hope of winning.

At the time of the Cairo meeting, I was convinced that Nasser did not want war. But he had no choice, for the determining factor was Tel Aviv's threat against Syria who, as we know, was bound to Egypt by that bilateral defense pact.

King Hussein was then asked: Why, if Nasser didn't want war, did he ask for the withdrawal of the U.N. Security Force? Was it a bluff in that he was convinced they would never withdraw?

I am certain that Nasser didn't want war. When he asked for the withdrawal of the U.N. forces from the demilitarized zone in Sinai, I thought rather that he wanted to normalize Egypt's rights over a territory that belonged to her in the first place.

I repeat that I was convinced Nasser did not want war. His back was to the wall; there was no other alternative. And even faced with the *fait accompli,* I am sure he didn't really believe war would break out. I imagine that he simply hoped to relieve the pressure on Syria. Clearly, it was a poor choice of tactics. It might have been better perhaps if he had deployed his forces in Sinai behind those of the U.N. and said: "If you attack Syria, we are ready."

It is true that he was proud of his military equipment, confident of the strength of his army, and sufficiently satisfied with the potential at his command to think he could hold his own against an aggressor. The proof of this is that Nasser never called on us. It was we who called on him.

After the Israeli-Arab conflict, there was a great deal of controversy over who should bear the responsibility for starting hostilities. Does an "act of aggression" necessarily involve the use of arms? Might not the closing of the Strait of Tiran be considered an "act of aggression"? What in fact is an "act of aggression"?

Basically, Tiran was only one of several weapons used in that atmosphere of hostility which, ever since the partition of 1947, plunged the Middle East into this tragedy we all suffer. Yes, Tiran was the trigger in a series of aggressive acts and reciprocal threats dating from 1948. That does not take away from the fact that Tiran was a mistake. I am well aware of it. Without question, we could have acted differently, even though the Arab action was but a reaction to Israeli threats. Like it or not, our reaction worked against us and gave Israel an excuse for attaining her ends. The Israelis had planned their maneuvers and we acted exactly as they hoped we would.

Finally, to get back to my May 30 trip to Egypt: even if there was still the same climate of belligerence between Arabs and Israelis, our position seemed less perilous because we had revived our system of military coordination with Nasser. We felt relieved, or at least I did. If only we could have had a little more time!

And so I left Cairo in the afternoon of this 30th of May. I once again took the controls of the ALIA Caravelle I had chartered only that morning and took off for Amman. I had had it! The day had been a good deal too long for me!

Shukairy was in the plane.

"What's this guy doing here. . . ?" one of the officers in the cabin started to ask.

I signaled him to shut up. I didn't want to hear any more. I had had enough for one day.

Since the meeting between Hussein and Nasser had been secret, it wasn't until the beginning of the afternoon of May 30—during a rerun of Radio-Cairo's broadcast of the official signing—that Jordan heard the news.

The anxiety of the Jordanian people in the face of a situation that was rapidly deteriorating and that seemed to be isolating Jordan from the rest of the Arab world changed to an enormous sigh of relief. The malaise which, since Es Samu, had strained relations between King Hussein and those Jordanians of Palestinian origin, suddenly vanished in an indescribable explosion of popular joy. This was so great that, as he emerged from the plane in Amman, the King was welcomed by thousands of demonstrators who had rushed in a few hours from every corner of Jordan. To emphasize their satisfaction, they repeatedly lifted his car in triumph.

Zeid Rifai, Chief of Protocol in the Royal Palace and private secretary to the King, explained the nature of this sudden change in Jordanian sentiment.

Rifai speaks:

After the signing of the treaty between Egypt and Jordan, Radio-Cairo announced the return of the King. This is how the Jordanians learned of his unexpected trip to Egypt. They came running by the thousands from everywhere, to welcome him and give him a triumphant reception. You must understand that to the man on the street, it seemed that the King had overcome the obstacles to Arab divisiveness. At the same time, he had succeeded in organizing Jordan's defense against the Israeli aggression we all considered imminent.

We were astonished to see Ahmed Shukairy leave the Caravelle behind the King. Bareheaded and dressed in a Mao-style khaki uniform, he seemed very sure of himself and came toward us with no sign of embarrassment, as if nothing was wrong, as if for him to land in Jordan was the most natural thing in the world. Mr. Shukairy had no doubt forgotten that for a year he had been proclaiming: "We must strike at the power of Amman before we take on Tel Aviv!" and "to liberate Tel Aviv, we must first free Amman." I pass over these, and worse. At the same time, the Palestine Liberation Organization delegate in Lebanon, Chafik El Hout, which means "the whale," was thundering: "Jordan is an integral part of Palestine, just like Israel!"

These considerations did not keep Mr. Shukairy from embracing a few here, and shaking hands with a few there. Finally, Prime Minister Saad Jumaa took him off to the Hotel Jordan Intercontinental.

But for all these protestations of friendship, we must not lose sight of the fact that King Hussein's meeting with Nasser was nothing more than a business conference, organized to salvage their common interests—those of the Arab world.

I know that the international press has used reams of

paper trying to explain what it called "the reconciliation of the enemy brothers." It was a lot of wasted ink. When the King and Nasser embraced each other as the King was leaving Cairo, it was nothing more than a traditional Arab gesture meaning that an agreement had been reached. On the other hand, the King never embraced Ahmed Shukairy.

[Author's note: We showed King Hussein a photograph from the front page of an important French daily with the caption: "The embrace of the enemy brothers." We pointed out that the caption seemed to suggest he was taking care to keep his hand within reach of his gun, while Nasser seemed to be trying to get at it.

The King found the interpretation very funny. He burst out laughing.]

Chapter 7
On the Eve of War

"All we had in Jordan was
a plan of defense."

The King speaks:

On June 1, 1967, General Abdel Moneim Riad, commander of the Arab forces on the Jordanian front, landed in Amman with his Egyptian General Staff. Riad had been assistant to the head of the United Arab Command. He was about 50, an experienced professional soldier and one of the best Arab generals. (After the June defeat, Nasser named him Chief of Staff of the Egyptian Armed Forces.*) In theory, he was also supposed to take command of the Iraqi, Saudi Arabian and Syrian troops and of two battalions of Egyptian commandos which, according to the agreements made with Nasser, were to reinforce our positions. This was what we had decided in Cairo.

We had reexamined the general lay of the land and concluded that our joint strategy required reinforcements so that there would be no break in the front shared by the three Arab countries neighboring on Israel.

On Saturday, June 3, at 2 P.M., I held a press conference with a hundred foreign and Jordanian correspondents in the Royal Palace at Amman. While the conference was in progress, I was called to the phone. It was Nasser in Cairo. I left the conference hall to pick up the call in my

* General Riad was fatally wounded in March 1969 by an Israeli shell while he was directing Egyptian artillery fire near the Suez Canal.

office. When our conversation was finished, I went back into the hall and announced:

"President Nasser has just informed me that Iraq has also signed the defense pact with Egypt. There are now four Arab states bound by this agreement. Iraqi troops will occupy designated positions along the Jordan-Israel border."

I had barely finished the sentence when an American journalist asked with that bluntness characteristic of Anglo-Saxon political correspondents:

"Do you anticipate war in the Middle East?"

I answered: "Yes."

"How soon do you think?"

"In the next 48 hours. If not, the Israelis will drop the idea, at least for the moment, in the hope of finding a more propitious time when our attention is diverted."

And I was convinced of what I said.

Moreover, my calculations turned out to be correct.

I had already alerted Nasser against an Israeli attack at our meeting in Cairo on May 30. I had explained my view that if Israel decided to attack, its first objective would be the Arab air forces, and that its first assault would quite naturally be directed against the Egyptian air force.

Nasser had answered:

"That's obvious. We expect it . . ."

I tried to alert everyone one last time on Sunday evening, June 4, through General Amer Khammash, Chief of Staff of the Jordanian Armed Forces, who expressed our anxiety to General Riad. In other words, we sounded the alarm once again to make clear that we expected a vast Israeli offensive at any moment.

That same Sunday evening, I ordered our air force to

place all its aircraft on alert and to be ready to protect all Jordanian airports, starting at dawn on the next day, Monday, June 5.

The afternoon and evening of that Sunday I spent in meetings with General Riad and my higher-ranking officers at Army Headquarters.

All we had in Jordan was a plan of defense. An offensive action was out of the question, particularly with the limited forces available at that time.

Then this statement was made to King Hussein: Concerning the Jordanian defense plan, Israeli intelligence stated that it seized documents from the staffs of several Jordanian regiments and that these documents—according to the Israelis—contained orders dated from the end of May which referred to plans for a Jordanian offensive against Israeli villages in the area of Latrun.

The King replied:

That is precisely one of the points I want to clear up.

Those Israeli villages were organized on two levels: civilian and military.

Following the Es Samu incident, we made certain preparations in case the Israelis were tempted to try further operations of that kind. Had this happened, we would have given them tit for tat, for top priority had been given to a selection of possible objectives of a paramilitary nature and retaliation would have been automatic. These preparations had nothing to do with the conflict of June 1967. It was this plan that the Israelis found and which, in their view, constituted an offensive against the Latrun area. Never have we contemplated an offensive against Israel! Given our relative strengths, it would have been madness.

That being the case, it wasn't until General Riad ar-

rived in Amman and we learned the exact potential of the
Iraqi forces joining ours that we were able to consider any
kind of strategy. We were still waiting for the Saudi
Arabian forces.

By then, it was the evening of Sunday, June 4. An
extraordinary meeting was called between General Riad,
his assistant, the Jordanian Chief of Staff, and the top
military command. It wasn't until this meeting that we
actually got down to studying the various opportunities
open to us. And we were already on the eve of the first day
of this so-called war!

So we decided to remain on the defensive along a very
limited front until the arrival of the Iraqi and Saudi
Arabian reinforcements when the front could be gradually
extended.

Buttressed by these reinforcements, we would then move
into the offensive phase of the operation. When I speak of
an offensive, I'm using a rather large word. The plan we
had hurriedly drawn up consisted of a few operations com-
bining air and artillery in the hope of neutralizing the
Israeli airports.

Had the Iraqis arrived in time, the situation would have
been much improved. Then we might have seen everything more clearly.

The fact is that the first part of an Iraqi brigade only
began to cross the Jordanian frontier that same Sunday
night. With them came a Palestinian battalion. This Palestine Liberation Organization battalion was really not
provided for in the agreement reached with Nasser in
Cairo. When these men in their leopard-spotted uniforms
began to arrive, the Jordanian officer at the border hesitated to let them through and telephoned Amman Head-

quarters where I happened to be. "Don't worry about it. Send them on their way as quickly as possible," I had them tell the officer.

I might mention in passing that these Iraqi and Palestinian troops never reached the positions Riad had assigned them, which were 200 kilometers from the Iraq-Jordan border they were crossing that night. Fighting began the next day, and as they were moving up to their positions, they were ruthlessly attacked and wiped out by Israeli planes.

Now to the question of Egyptian reinforcements. On Saturday afternoon, June 3, eleven troop transports of the United Arab Republic arrived with parts of two battalions of Egyptian commandos (the 33d and the 53d). On Sunday afternoon, June 4, I welcomed the rest of the Egyptian detachment at the Amman airport.

Once again, we were too late. These commandos, whose assignment was to join ours on the west bank of the Jordan, were still not at their posts on Monday when the so-called war broke out.

On this same Sunday, Riad had made me see that our effective land force of 56,000 men was not enough to defend a front stretching 650 kilometers along our border with Israel. As for our armored potential, it consisted only of 176 Patton M.48's, the remainder being light-weight equipment.

After considering various solutions, Riad said:

"The Syrian front can easily be held by a third of the Syrian forces. As I see it, the Syrians can carry out their assignment with only five of their 15 brigades. I suggest you ask them immediately to send their 10 reserve brigades to bolster our front."

I accepted the Egyptian General's proposal even though I had few illusions about the possibility of aid from Damascus. The truth is that up to then, the Syrians had systematically refused to cooperate with us. That is why Riad then suggested:

"Do I have your approval to send Marshal Amer [Vice-President and Commander in Chief of the U.A.R. forces] a message asking him to give the request his official backing in Damascus? Even if it's only for the history books . . . or the record, whichever you prefer . . ." Riad added.

I agreed:

"All right, if you think it necessary . . ."

That same night, thanks to our network of military transmitters, we were able to inform the Syrians of our request for reinforcements. They never answered. It wouldn't be fair to say the Syrians never helped us. No . . . On Wednesday, June 7, while this so-called war was coming to an end so far as Jordan was concerned, Syria sent us one brigade. This brigade reached Suweilih, a Jordanian village about 60 kilometers from the Syrian border. It was as near as it got to the field of battle. When they heard that the Syrian plains were now under attack, they turned around and headed for home with no further explanation.

I conferred very late that Sunday with General Riad. At one in the morning I decided to go home to bed. There was nothing more to do but wait.

I have to admit that that Sunday night was one of the worst I have ever spent. I had great trouble getting to sleep and even more difficulty staying asleep.

Chapter 8
Israel's Great Offensive

"It was now 9 A.M. on Monday, June 5, and
we were at war."

The King speaks:

At dawn on Monday, June 5, our air force began its task
of protecting Jordan's skies.

At 8:50, fully dressed—I realized that for 10 days I had
been wearing battle dress exclusively—I was waiting for
breakfast with my wife. The telephone rang and I picked
up the receiver. It was my chief aide-de-camp, Colonel
Jazy:

"Your Majesty, the Israeli offensive has begun in Egypt.
It's just been announced by Radio-Cairo."

That is how I learned of the start of hostilities.

I immediately contacted headquarters which confirmed
the news at about 9 A.M. Orders in code from Marshal
Abdel Hakim Amer, Commander of the Egyptian Armed
Forces in Cairo, had just come over the direct line linking
us with General Riad.

The message was as follows:

1. Israeli planes have started to bomb air bases of the
U.A.R. and approximately 75 per cent of the enemy's aircraft have been destroyed or put out of action.

2. The counterattack by the Egyptian air force was
underway over Israel. In Sinai, U.A.R. troops have engaged the enemy and taken the offensive on the ground.

3. As a result, Marshal Amer has ordered the Commander in Chief of the Jordanian front to open a new front and to launch offensive operations according to the plan outlined the day before.

Without touching my breakfast, I jumped behind the wheel of my car and headed for Army Headquarters. Once there, I exchanged my car for a military jeep equipped with a two-way radio.

In the blockhouse in the headquarters basement, I carefully examined Marshal Amer's message under the neon lights and then conferred with Riad on what moves had already been made.

"I've given our artillery orders to occupy the front lines," he said. "An infantry battalion of the Imam Ali brigade has been ordered to occupy Mount Scopus in Jerusalem."

Mount Scopus is in the demilitarized zone of Jerusalem. The headquarters of the Norwegian General, Odd Bull, Chief of Staff of the U.N. Security Force, have been in this isolated spot since the first Israeli-Arab conflict in 1948.

Mount Scopus was occupied by our troops a short time later.

Riad then gave our Hawker Hunters the green light. Their mission, together with the Iraqi and Syrian air forces, was to bomb Israeli air bases in the hope of neutralizing as much as possible the efficiency of the enemy air force.

The night before, we had barely had the time to tick off the operational pilots we could count on. Some of our men were in the United States completing their training. At this point, we had only 16 pilots for a fleet of 22 Hawker Hunters. No wonder we were unable to plan any large-scale aerial maneuvers without the help of Iraqi and Syrian planes!

It must be remembered that our weakness in men and airplanes was due to the fact that the June '67 conflict found us in the midst of organizing our air force. It became yet another casualty of this fiasco which swamped our efforts to establish a common Arab defense system. It was to have taken us three years; we had 15 months to go. The responsibility for all this, I repeat, falls in great measure on the ill-advised actions of the P.L.O. which, whether it meant to or not, sabotaged everything.

It is not for me to judge, but I have the right to acknowledge a fact.

In the course of the organization of our air force, we were to receive 36 Starfighters F 104 from the United States.

During the training period, one pilot was killed in an F 104 in the United States and a second crashed with his trainer here in Jordan. We might recall that similar accidents in F 104's took place in West Germany.

Be that as it may, at the beginning of June, six F 104's were stationed in Amman with a team of American instructors who were carrying out a program of military assistance signed in Washington. We had insured these planes with a Lebanese-Swiss insurance company. However, our contract did not cover war risks.* Also, a few days before the start of the conflict, we realized that these F 104 trainers (loaned to us by the United States) could present a grave risk if they were caught on the ground, so I asked the Americans to take them out of Jordan. But they turned

---

* Jordan is the only country in the world—together with the Sudan—which insures its military aircraft.

a deaf ear. They contended that our fears were groundless. Finally, when they saw that we didn't have a single pilot capable of flying these six Starfighters, they came around. On Sunday afternoon, June 4, the Americans decided to relieve us of our burden, barely escaping the rockets of the Israeli Mirages.

It was now 9 A.M. on Monday, June 5, and we were at war.

Riad increased our fire power against the Israeli air bases by directing our heavy artillery—long-range 155's— on the Israeli air force installations within our line of fire. Our field artillery also went into action, and our Hawker Hunters were ready to take part in the combined operation with the Iraqi and Syrians.

The King was asked: Why didn't the Jordanian pilots take off right away?

We were waiting for the Syrians. Without the help of their Migs, the bombing of the Israeli bases would have had a negligible effect.

The operations center of our air force had been in contact with the Syrians since 9 A.M. They said they had been caught off guard: their aircraft were not ready for the strike, and their fighter pilots were on a training flight. They asked us to give them first a half-hour, then an hour, and so on until 10:45 when they asked for yet another delay which we also granted. At 11 o'clock, we couldn't wait any longer. The Iraqis had already taken off and were on their way to join us. The result of these repeated Syrian postponements was that our operation did not really get off the ground until well after 11 A.M.

I remember that, at that moment, an observer from a

friendly country who was following developments in our operations center took me aside. He advised me to assemble all the air equipment we couldn't use and send it outside Jordan to preserve it from a probable Israeli air raid.

The equipment referred to included:

2 D.C. 7's belonging to ALIA
2 English helicopters (1 Scout and 1 S. 55)
1 twin-engine American Cessna for training
1 U.N. D.C. 3
1 English Chipmunk for training
1 Heron (English transport)
2 French helicopters, Alouette 111's
(the only planes preserved from the carnage, thanks to their pilots' bravery.)

All evidence indicated that this was a sensible idea. The threat to these sitting ducks was clear. Yet I found it hard to make the decision and hesitated to send the planes off in such a hurry.

It was at this point that we received a telephone call at Air Force Headquarters from U.N. General Odd Bull. It was a little after 11 A.M.

The Norwegian General informed me that the Israeli Prime Minister had addressed an appeal to Jordan. Mr. Eshkol had summarily announced that the Israeli offensive had started that morning, Monday, June 5, with operations directed against the United Arab Republic, and then he added: "If you don't intervene, you will suffer no consequences."

By this time we were already fighting in Jerusalem and our planes had just taken off to bomb Israeli air bases. So I answered Odd Bull:

1. "The Enemy Brothers' Embrace": Hussein and Nasser greet each other in Cairo, May 30, 1967. *(Photo by U.P.)*

2. The signing of the common defense pact between Jordan and Egypt in Cairo, May 30, 1967. Shukairy sits at King Hussein's right. At Nasser's left, his two vice-presidents, Marshal Abdel Hakim Amer, his "dauphin" and Commander in Chief of the Egyptian Armed Forces, who, according to rumor, committed suicide following the defeat of June 1967

3. The King with, on his right, the Egyptian General Ali Amer, head of the United Arab Command, and on his left, General Habes Majali, Commander in Chief of the Jordanian Arab Legion.

4. On the eve of the June, 1967 war, the King makes a tour of the mess halls in the Jordan Valley. On his right, his cousin Sherif Zeid Ben Chaker, commander of the 60th tank brigade. On his left, his maternal uncle, Sherif Nasser Ben Jamil, one of the two assistants assigned to General Habes Majali, Commander in Chief of the Jordanian army.

5. The King at Jordanian Headquarters during the Six-Day War. On his right, General Amer Khammash. Behind him, in civilian clothes, his personal secretary and chief of protocol at the Royal Palace, Zeid Rifai. (Photo by Charles Gerretsen)

6. The war is lost. Exhausted and broken in spirit, the King addresses his people. *(Photo by Charles Courrière)*

7. Hussein of Jordan visits Russia for the first time in his attempt to enlist the Great Powers' help in a search for peace. Face to face with the Soviet leaders and the Arabs' allies, the King and his entourage sit smiling. *(Photo by A. Floutu)*

8/9. In Amman: the funeral procession of the commandos killed in Karameh, Thursday, March 21, 1968, during the course of the Israeli "police action." At the head of the procession, a "mini-commando," son of one of the victims.

10/11/12. In Shune, the King on
Israeli tank in which the drive
corpse was found. The same tank is
on exhibit in Amman, barely visi
under the cluster of curious Jordania

"They started the battle. Well, they are receiving our reply by air." *

Three times, our Hawker Hunters attacked the bases at Natanya in Israel without a loss. And our pilots reported that they destroyed four enemy planes on the ground, the only ones they had seen.

On their side, the Iraqis bombed the airport at Lydda. And a little later, the Syrians finally headed for the base at Ramt David and the refineries in Haifa.

Since I believe that the only value in an error is the lesson learned, I would like to make clear here—without pinning the responsibility on any one in particular—that two actions at the start of the conflict cost us Arabs much.

First, the unfortunate delay of the Syrian air force made us miss an important opportunity to turn things to our advantage. Had it not been for the Syrians' procrastination, we could have started the bombing of Israel earlier. Then we could easily have intercepted the Israeli bombers returning from their raids on Egypt empty of ammunition and fuel, or we might even have surprised them on the ground as they were being refueled. It's not unthinkable that this alone might have modified the outcome.

And then—it isn't fair to place all the blame on the Syrians—we were misinformed about what had happened in Egypt when the Israelis attacked the U.A.R. air bases. A new message from Marshal Amer informed us that the Israeli air offensive was continuing. But at the same time,

* Two days later, on Wednesday morning, June 7, the Israeli Minister of Defense, Moshe Dayan, answered King Hussein's request for a negotiated cease-fire in the same biting tone: "We have been offering the King an opportunity to cut his losses ever since Monday morning. Now we have 500 dead and wounded in Jerusalem. So, tell him that from now on, I'll talk to him only with the gunsights of our tanks!"

he insisted that the Egyptians had put 75 per cent of the Israeli air force out of action! The same message said that U.A.R. bombers had destroyed the Israeli bases in a counterattack, and that the ground forces of the Egyptian army had penetrated into Israel by way of the Negev!

These reports—fantastic to say the least—had much to do with our confusion and false interpretation of the situation. To such a degree that, when a little later, our radar screen showed planes flying from Egypt toward Israel, we didn't give it a thought. We simply assumed they were from the U.A.R. air force on their way to a mission over Israel. They weren't. They were Israeli bombers on the way home, their first mission against Egypt accomplished!

Ignorant of the truth and vaguely reassured, I left Air Force Headquarters for General Riad's when our first squadron of Hawker Hunters returned from Israel, soon followed by a second. Not one of our planes had been touched or forced down during their raids.

A brief exchange with the pilots confirmed my fears about what future operations our men could undertake. Our pilots had no idea what they were supposed to do. Obviously, they were quick to obey orders. But that was where the trouble lay. The orders we gave them were very brief, because our lack of intelligence prevented us from making them more detailed. Therefore they had to improvise. Unlike the Israeli flyers, they lacked precise information that would make it possible to follow a carefully thought-out plan to the last detail. Thanks to Israeli intelligence, their pilots knew exactly what to expect. It was revealed by Israeli authorities after the June conflict that their pilots had a complete catalogue of the most minute details of each of the 32 Arab air bases, what objectives to strike, where, when and how. We had nothing like that.

And that is how this so-called war stood when I decided to leave Air Force Headquarters to find General Riad.

Then started our misfortunes!

No sooner had I arrived at Army Headquarters at 12:30 than the first wave of Israeli planes dropped its bombs on the Amman airport.

Chapter 9
The Israeli Attempt
on Hussein's Life

At 12:30 on that 5th of June came the first Israeli response to the combined bombing by the Jordanians, Iraqis and Syrians. One of the Mirages' objectives was the military airport at Amman. It was during this bombing that the Israeli attempt on the King of Jordan's life took place. Hussein refused to speak of the incident:

"I can't tell you a thing. I didn't see it. Besides, it isn't important."

Zeid Rifai, Chief of Protocol at the Royal Palace, was a witness.

Rifai speaks:

It was 1:10 P.M. A second wave of Israeli bombers attacked the Amman airport, 40 minutes after the first one. It lasted until 3:30. We didn't have a single aircraft left. The Israelis caught them all by surprise as they were taking on fresh ammunition and fuel. They were destroyed on the ground before they could take off.

I was at the Royal Palace. Most of the staff had taken refuge in the shelters. From time to time, the sound of muffled explosions reached my office and the windows rattled. My assistant, Motassem Bilbeissi, and I couldn't stand the confinement any longer so we decided to go out and see what was happening. Two soldiers stood guard at the top of the steps with fixed bayonets. They were wearing the red and white checked *schmagh* of the Arab Legion on their heads.

As we reached the steps, the explosions made us turn our heads toward the Amman airport, which was capped with heavy dark gray smoke. From where we were standing, we could see the Israeli fighter bombers drop a load of rockets, fly toward us, bank and turn back to drop another load on the airport. As they banked over our heads, they were flying so low that I could see not only the pilots' silhouettes but also their expressions of astonishment, as if they were wondering what the devil we were doing there at such a moment.

At 2:30, the Israeli raid seemed to be coming to an end. An awesome silence spread over the seven hills of Amman. The silence was even more unbearable. There was nothing left but the excruciating silence and the spirals of heavy gray smoke rising above the airport. We wanted to see the extent of the damage, so Bilbeissi and I jumped into my car. As I was turning on the switch, he touched my arm and made me a sign to look up. Planes. This time they weren't going into a turn but coming straight for us. We counted 12 of them. Twelve Mystères. Suddenly, five swerved toward the south, five toward the north [the Amman airport was east and the Royal Palace west], and the last two dropped toward us.

"Let's get out of the car," I hurriedly said to Bilbeissi. "They're heading for the palace!"

At that moment, the first Mystère was hit by the palace's antiaircraft. Its right wing on fire, the plane lurched and plunged toward the north where it crashed.

The second plane swept down, grazing the trees that

screened the windows of His Majesty's private office. Its first rocket exploded against the wall next to one of the windows. Immediately after, a second penetrated the conference hall. The Mystère was up and banking toward the north when it came full circle and headed back to the palace at full speed. This time, it machine-gunned the King's office at point-blank range with a precision and knowledge of its target that was stupefying. Then, finally, it disappeared.

The two sentinels at the top of the steps never left their posts. With no shelter and furious that any one should dare make an attempt on the King's life, they alternately fired bullets and obscenities at the Israeli fighter.

I went over to assess the damage. The wall behind the desk and King's chair was lacerated by the blast. Bilbeissi and I stood rooted: His Majesty could have been there so easily; he could hardly have escaped the Mystère's machine guns.

I returned to my office and telephoned the King at Army Headquarters.

I said: "The palace was hit, but nothing serious. Your Majesty has no need to worry."

The King only asked if any one had been wounded.

"No, Sire, no one."

"In that case, it's all right," he calmly said, and hung up.

Chapter 10

The Jordanian Air Force Is Wiped Out

"At Mafraq, only the mess hall was left standing."

The King speaks again:

On Monday, June 5, a few moments after the first Israeli raid on Amman, I received the first telephone call from Nasser since the start of hostilities.

The President of the U.A.R. began by repeating what Marshal Amer had already told us that morning: "Israel bombed our air bases. We answered by bombing hers. We are launching a general offensive in the Negev."

Then he asked me quickly to take possession of the largest possible amount of land in order to get ahead of the U.N.'s cease-fire. "For," he said, "I've been informed that the Security Council is intervening tonight to stop the war."

I had no idea that Nasser was in such a weak position. I was to learn that later.

At 2:30, the Israelis left after having literally smashed our air bases to a pulp—the only ones we had, at Amman and at Mafraq, 90 kilometers from Amman on the road to Damascus and Baghdad. It was obvious that their principal objective had been to make the landing fields unusable. While they were at it, they also took care of our fleet of Hawker Hunters.

Most of our aircraft were back from their mission over Israel and were being refueled. Before they knew what hit them, our pilots saw their planes pulverized by an avalanche of Israeli rockets. Two of them were still in the air and engaged the enemy.

At the military base in Mafraq, Major Firass Ajlouni, who an hour earlier had led his squadron in the attack on the Israeli airports, was on the point of taking off. A wave of Israeli bombers appeared and raked the air strip with rockets, quickly followed by a second wave of Mirages. Without a moment's hesitation, Firass Ajlouni revved up his Hawker Hunter to get into the air and fight. But just as his plane was leaving the ground, he received a full burst and crashed. Firass Ajlouni was killed. He was 27 and one of our best pilots. He was the only Jordanian aviator to lose his life in the so-called war. Today, a square in Amman bears his name.*

* Of mixed Bedhouin and Circasian birth, Ajlouni had been an athlete, a bachelor, and mad about sports and flying. He belonged to that "elite group of the King's beloved children," who were the air force pilots of Jordan. After leaving the military academy in Amman, he continued his training in England. He had always had a premonition that he would die in a plane or at war. And he did both. His father was a senator and had been Jordanian Minister of Defense after starting out as a general in the Ottoman army.

Firass Ajlouni had always sworn to avenge the death of his best friend, Lieutenant Mouwafak Salti (married to an English girl, and a father), who was a Jordanian pilot of 26, killed accidentally during an Israeli-Arab incident over the Dead Sea soon after the raid on Es Samu. Lieutenant Salti's plane was shot down by an Israeli fighter as he was trying to protect a friend—Lt. Ehsan Chourdom—who was in serious difficulties. Lt. Salti used his ejector seat but his parachute failed to open.

Perhaps the initiator of this "chain of friendship," Lt. Chourdom wanted to avenge his comrades during the June conflict. He shot down one Mirage, two Mystères and a Vautour over the H. 3 base in Iraq on Wednesday, June 7.

Some of our Hawker Hunters were returning from their third mission over Israel and got caught in the middle of the bombing. Unable to land, they were shot down. Another violent battle broke out over the base at Mafraq. Four Mirages were destroyed. But our planes were so overwhelmed by the number and superior quality of the enemy aircraft that, one by one, they were forced down. One of our Hawker Hunters held off three Mirages but finally ran out of ammunition and crashed.

For all the heroism of our pilots, our newborn air force from then on was out of action.

And that was the first day's score card.

Our commander on the western front was given orders to occupy the advance posts with his batteries of long-range 155's. Beginning at 5 P.M., they were to bombard, at intervals of ten minutes, the following enemy objectives: the radar station at El Kastal and the air bases at Kfar Cirkin, Ein Shamer, Mijiddo and Kapool.

At the end of the afternoon, I went to inspect the Amman airport and the military hospital to see for myself what had happened. Then, at 9:30 P.M., I took the road for the base at Mafraq.

At Mafraq, only the mess hall was left standing.

At the military hospital, I talked with each pilot, including those who were wounded during the Israeli counteroffensive against our air bases. I remember a boy who kept complaining. I went over to him to find out what was the matter and to try to comfort him. I asked him if his wound hurt, and he answered:

"It isn't that that bothers me so much, but I've lost my second finger. I'll never be able to use a machine gun again!"

Another pilot was beside himself because he hadn't taken part in the fight. In point of fact, I had forced him to stay in the hospital three days before for an attack of kidney stones which was causing him excruciating pain.

I called together the 14 pilots who were left and told them:

"All our planes are destroyed. You are to leave immediately with your ground crews to put yourself at the Iraqi's disposal before the war ends." *

It was I who organized their departure during the night by the only means of transportation still available—a military bus. They made it to the Iraqi base H. 3, which is not far from the reference point H. 3 on the pipe line that lies athwart the Jordan-Iraq border. On their arrival, they were given some Hawker Hunters. Three of our pilots brought down nine enemy aircraft during the Israeli attack on H. 3, including Mystères, and three Mirages, in spite of the absence of adequate radar which forced them to fly blind.

One captain (now a major), Ehsan Chourdom, alone destroyed one Mirage, two Mystères and a Vautour on the way back from bombing H. 3. Since the Mirages were much faster and better armed than the Hawker Hunters, Chourdom waited until they returned from their mission flying slowly with almost empty tanks. This way, the odds would favor him. During one of the engagements, Captain Chourdom went to help a beleaguered friend. He brought

* Only two planes escaped the massacre: two Alouette 111 helicopters which were on the Amman airfield at the time of the Israeli attack. The one reserved for the King was evacuated during the raid by its 26-year-old pilot, Lt. Awni Maher, and placed out of harm's way under the brow of the hill where the military base and the civilian airport of Amman are situated.

down one of the Israeli planes, but as he was about to go after the second, his machine gun jammed. The Israeli plane took advantage of his plight, moved away and disappeared.

Our pilots continued to do their best. On Wednesday, June 7, the day of the cease-fire, six Israeli planes again attacked the Iraqi base at H. 3. Our pilots brought down four. Two Israeli pilots were killed and two taken prisoner.

Chapter 11

The Destruction
of Jordan's Tanks

"From Monday evening to Tuesday morning . . .
that night was hell."

The King continues:

Throughout that first day, our batteries of long-range 155's kept pounding at the outskirts of Tel Aviv, its concentration of military targets, and the airport at Lydda.

But I cannot pass over in silence the tactical error we made in the movement of our tanks, for the consequences were as disastrous as the loss of our air force.

I must explain:

Our tank force was divided into two brigades of Patton M. 48's, the 40th and the 60th.

The first, under the command of Colonel Rakan Anad, was stationed on the northern front, meaning the northern section of the Jordan valley and the northwestern part of the country. The second brigade, under the command of my cousin, Sherif Zeid Chaker, was defending the southern end of the Jordan valley and the rear flank behind Jerusalem. Their position was dictated by the armistice treaty of 1949 which stipulated that tanks must stay at a certain distance from the Holy City.

It all began with the first maneuver decided upon at 1 P.M. that Monday. The 40th brigade, holding the northern front, was to take the place of the 60th defending the

Jericho sector. At 12:40, Riad had ordered the 60th to move toward Hebron in order to reach Beersheba, which was the most important Israeli tank base. The initial aim of this maneuver was to join forces with the first Egyptian units which were supposedly reaching the advance posts on the southern front at any moment.

Essential to the success of this operation was the immediate arrival of Syrian reinforcements on the northern front. We were counting on these to plug the gap left by the departure of our 40th brigade. Admittedly, we should have left our tanks where they were, knowing perfectly well that Israel would not miss an opportunity to use the breach to move toward the north and invade the valley, thereby isolating the two banks of the Jordan. It was for this very reason that we had originally concentrated the two tank brigades on the northern and southern fronts in a pincer movement that would literally lock up Israel's means of access to the Jordan.

As soon as the 40th received Riad's new instructions, it started on its way south, without air cover—we were already unable to provide any—and under constant harassment from Israeli planes. During the course of the trip, our Pattons managed to bring down four of them.

At the moment the 40th was finally nearing the outskirts of Jericho, the Iraqi brigade and the Palestinian battalion were desperately trying to reach Irbid and Jerash in order to take up their positions in the Jordan valley, which was in dire need of reinforcements. The Iraqis didn't reach the valley until the very end of the conflict, and by the time they got there, the brigade had been reduced to almost nothing by the constant pounding of the Israeli aircraft.

As for our 40th brigade, it managed, despite enemy interference, to take up its position in Jericho and relieve the 60th as ordered.

At the same time, Israeli tanks, supported by their air force, opened a large-scale offensive on the northern front in the area of Jenin where we had only one infantry brigade (the "Khaled Ibn El Walid"), one tank squadron of Pattons and, of course, no air support. In spite of the odds against us, the battle was violent. We managed several times to repulse the Israelis, and they lost 17 tanks in the first engagement. In the face of our resistance, the Israeli tanks began to withdraw. Seeing this, our tanks swept boldly out of their emplacements to give chase. That was a mistake! No sooner was our squadron out in the open than the Israelis raked it over the coals. The price of this tactical error was the squadron's complete destruction. When the cease-fire was declared, little remained of the Khaled Ibn El Walid brigade either.

At this point, General Riad pressed the Syrians to come and relieve us from Israeli pressure on the northern front. They refused, claiming they could do nothing without air support.

At 7:15 P.M., Riad sent a message to General Fawzi, Chief of Staff of the United Command, telling him that the enemy had penetrated into the area around Jenin toward Nablus, that the situation in Jenin was critical, and that we desperately needed Syrian and Iraqi air support.

Then at 8:45 P.M., past desperation, he ordered the 40th which was fighting in Jericho to turn back and head north, and told the 60th to hold its position but to send some of its units to Jerusalem where the battle was at its height.

At 9:30 P.M., the 40th brigade left Jericho and charged as fast as possible (40 km. an hour) toward the north under a hail of Israeli rockets. When they reached Jenin, our tanks threw themselves into battle without even stopping to refuel.

All these movements had been dictated by General Riad and the top Jordanian officers in Amman.*

From Monday evening to Tuesday morning, I shuttled between Headquarters, the front, and all the places where my men were fighting.

That night was hell. It was as clear as day. The sky and the earth glowed with the light of the rockets and the constant explosions of the bombs pouring from Israeli planes.

---

* King Hussein, it is clear, did not wish to blame General Riad. However, as will be seen further on, the Egyptian general appointed by Nasser to command the Jordanian front was, according to Wasfi al Tall, solely responsible for these self-contradictory and confused maneuvers.

Chapter 12
The Collapse

"For me, this so-called war was lost."

The King was asked:

When did you realize that, for all Egypt's intoxication, the situation was not what Cairo wanted you to believe, and that the outcome of the war had already been decided?

At 2 P.M. on Tuesday, June 6, the situation was perfectly clear. For me, this so-called war was lost. One, our air force had been out of commission since the day before. Two, our one and only radar—of English make—stationed on Mount Ajlun to the north of Amman near Jerash, was almost completely destroyed. The little it could do was either useless or difficult to decipher. In any case, and I can't explain why, the few bits of information we were able to pick up on the radar, such as where the Iraqi troops were, were regularly broadcast over "The Arab Voice" from Radio-Cairo. They believed they were doing a good thing in Cairo. Undoubtedly they thought it was a good way to stimulate morale in the rear. Whatever the reason, all the Israelis needed to do—and they did not forgo the pleasure—was to listen to "The Arab Voice" in order to subvert our efforts without the slightest risk. From the second day of the conflict, they bombed everything that moved, and, in particular, the area between the field of battle and the airports at H. 3 and Habaniyeh, near Baghdad.

Three: the tactical blunder we committed with our tanks cost us most of our armored force.

The result of all this was that by 2 P.M. on Tuesday, we were in such a desperate situation that we considered calling for a cease-fire that night.

At dawn on Tuesday, the second day of the war, the conflict had become purely defensive so far as we were concerned. The order of the day was: "HOLD ON."

Around 5:30 that morning, General Riad offered me the following options: try for a cease-fire through diplomatic channels, or order an immediate retreat so as to fall back at dusk to the east bank of the Jordan. Riad added:

"If we don't decide within the next 24 hours, you can kiss your army and all of Jordan good-by! We are on the verge of losing the west bank; all our forces will be isolated or destroyed."

We were at Army Headquarters. I thought for a moment, then asked the Egyptian general to consult Nasser to find out what he thought.

At that moment, the Israeli bombing attacks reached their climax.

Half an hour later, around 6 o'clock, Riad got through to Nasser. He explained the situation and put me through to the U.A.R. President from Civil Defense Headquarters where I had gone in the meanwhile. As usual, the conversation took place over the regular public telephone system. It could easily have been otherwise, since the United Arab Command had at its disposal an ultramodern system of transmission. But it had not anticipated the need. The equipment sat in Cairo.

This time Nasser's voice sounded a little anxious. Our conversation was mostly about the situation in the air and the suspected foreign intervention which Radio-Cairo had made much of during its first bulletins at 4:20 and 6:20 A.M.

It was this conversation between Nasser and me that the Israelis picked up without our knowledge, and edited and broadcast to the four winds.

This is the Israeli transcript of the telephone conversation they heard and recorded:

NASSER: How are you? I understand that His Majesty, our brother, wants to know if we are fighting on all fronts [garbled passage] . . . should we also announce that the United States is collaborating with Israel? . . . Hello! Hello! Don't hang up! I can't hear you . . . The connection is very poor. [Silence.] Hello! Should we say the United States and Britain, or only the United States?

HUSSEIN: The United States and Britain.

NASSER: Does Great Britain have aircraft carriers?

HUSSEIN: [Garbled answer.]

NASSER: Good. King Hussein will publish a communiqué on this and I'll publish the same communiqué.

HUSSEIN: Thank you.

NASSER: Don't give up.

HUSSEIN: All right.

NASSER: Hello! Hello! Brother, do not worry. You must be strong.

HUSSEIN: Yes, Mr. President, I understand. If you have any ideas, no matter what . . .

NASSER: We will fight with everything we have. We fought

on all fronts, all night. If we had a few problems at
the beginning, so what? We'll come out of it all right.
God is on our side [garbled passage] . . . So, Your
Majesty will publish a communiqué on the American
and English intervention.

HUSSEIN: [Inaudible answer.]

NASSER: As God is my witness, I tell you that I shall publish a communiqué and that you will publish a communiqué. And we'll see to it that the Syrians also
announce that American and English aircraft are
attacking us from their aircraft carriers. So, we will
publish this communiqué. We'll really emphasize this
point and we'll do it together.

HUSSEIN: Good, perfect.

NASSER: Your Majesty, do you agree?

HUSSEIN: [Garbled answer.]

NASSER: A thousand thanks. Don't give up. We are with
you with all our hearts. We dispatched our planes
against Israel today. Our planes have been bombing
the Israeli airports since early morning.

HUSSEIN: A thousand thanks. Stay well.

*King Hussein was asked: How did this idea of the
Anglo-American intervention arise?*

This business of the American-British intervention has
been given several different and obviously false interpretations. Which is not surprising. You can't blame people
for accepting a false explanation of something they didn't
actually see. Now, since I'm offered the chance, I would
like to clear up this affair.

As early as Monday morning, June 5, our air force

center reported that our radar had picked up some planes in two areas over the Mediterranean, 40 kilometers north of Bardaweel, and northeast of Port Said. According to this report, these unidentified planes disappeared from the screen on a line with the airport at Lydda in Israel.

Moreover, the radar picked up some stationary objects in the Mediterranean. And, according to this same report, the radar showed planes flying at sea level in the region of these stationary objects toward Israel. The conclusion drawn from this was that these planes were carrier-based. And we knew for a certainty that Israel had no ships of this type.

Of course, radar can't tell a plane's nationality.

Our confusion was increased by the fact that the Egyptian information on the number of Israeli planes already destroyed made it difficult to believe there were so many enemy planes still able to fly. Therefore, in making a correct evaluation of Israeli air power on the basis of our allies' information, the size of this air fleet seemed excessive unless a foreign country was involved.

And then, another thing that contributed to our confusion was the confusion of some of our pilots. These men said that they had seen Israeli fighters with the same silhouette as ours. Only one explanation was possible: these Hawker Hunters, a type of plane not in the Israeli arsenal, could only come from a base near the Middle East.

Later on, we learned that they were not Hawker Hunters but Israeli Mystères whose silhouettes are very similar. To illustrate this, I must cite a particularly eloquent case: it appears that one of our motorized units in the front lines allowed itself to be attacked by Israeli fighters without returning fire because our soldiers mistook the Mystères for our own Hawker Hunters.

Also later on, an investigation of our radar's strange reports led us to the hypothetical conclusion that in certain atmospheric conditions over the sea, a radar screen can easily reflect objects hard to identify—such as ships—which are really beyond its range although they appear to be near objects within the scope.

During the war, I encountered ambassadors from various foreign powers several times at our Civil Defense Headquarters in Amman. I sent Nasser a telegram telling him that the United States Ambassador had assured me that there was no American involvement of any kind in this conflict. But I must admit that at the time I wasn't convinced.

From the very beginning, I told all those in positions of responsibility, General Riad included, that the most important thing in this story was to determine the truth: did Israel wage this war alone, with only her own equipment, or did she have help from the outside? Whatever the truth is, it must serve to teach us a lesson.

From the beginning to the end of the conflict, I told my officers over and over again that the most serious abdication of our responsibilities, the error with the worst consequences, would be to cover over our mistakes and our weaknesses from ourselves and from others. Truth demanded that everyone know. That is why the American denial was immediately broadcast over Radio-Amman.

I have always insisted on the truth in everything. To me, there is nothing more important than truth and honesty. The Israelis have alleged that I "admitted" that this story of the Anglo-American intervention was a complete fabrication.

This is not true.

I really believed in America and England's intervention. When I stated it publicly, I believed it.

Chapter 13
The Jordanian Retreat

"It was like a dream, or worse
yet, like a nightmare."

King Hussein continues:

To get back to that famous Tuesday morning conversation with Nasser, I also talked to him about the situation on the Jordanian front, which Riad had just explained.

As a result, on Nasser's suggestion, Riad sent off to Cairo a coded cable saying:

"The situation on the west bank is becoming desperate. The Israelis are attacking on all fronts. We are bombed day and night by the Israeli air force and can offer no resistance because the major part of our combined air power has been put out of commission.

"Therefore, we now have three possible solutions:

"1. We can call for a political solution in the hope of bringing hostilities to an immediate end. This solution must come from a foreign source—the United States, Soviet Russia, or the U.N. Security Council.

"2. We can evacuate the west bank tonight.

"3. Or, obviously, we can try to stay on the west bank another 24 hours. But if we do, the total destruction of the Jordanian army is inevitable.

"King Hussein has asked me to inform you of the above in order to learn your opinion and your decision at the earliest possible time."

At 12:30 I sent a personal telegram to Nasser to back up Egyptian General Riad's message. Among other things, I told him:

"The situation is deteriorating rapidly. In Jerusalem it is critical. In addition to our very heavy losses in men and equipment, for lack of air protection, our tanks are being disabled at the rate of one every ten minutes. And the bulk of the enemy forces are concentrated against the Jordanian army.

"General Riad must have already told you all this in his message. I only hope that you will give us your views as soon as possible."

At almost the same moment, Riad received an answer from Marshal Amer in Cairo saying:

"We agree to the retreat from the west bank, and the arming of the civilian population."

I answered myself with another message:

"We are still holding on. We are trying to put off the retreat as long as possible. The civilian population has been armed for a long time."

I won't soon forget that Tuesday, June 6, the second day of the so-called war.

We clung like the demented to the west bank of the Jordan. Everywhere—in Jerusalem, in Ramallah, Hebron, around Nablus—we resisted in hand-to-hand combat, from trench to trench, from house to house, on the roofs, in the cellars. We even fought for fences! Proof of the bitter fighting was later given by the Israelis themselves. They said that the battle with Jordan was more violent than on any other Arab front. This may explain our heavy losses for the three days our war lasted—6,094 dead or missing.

During the course of that afternoon, I left Amman

Headquarters for the Jordan valley. I wanted to see the situation for myself. This was not unusual for me. My jeep had a two-way radio so that I could stay in constant touch with the Chief of Staff in Amman and at the same time follow operations on the spot as well as those on other parts of the front. I took the wheel because it let me concentrate more calmly on what was taking place. I have to admit that once June was over, it took me a long time to understand, digest and face up to what had happened. It was like a dream, or worse yet, like a nightmare.

So far as I'm concerned, to go through such an event, cooped up in a Chief of Staff's room, was one of the worst experiences I've ever undergone. I far and away prefer to be with my soldiers. There, I'm reassured because I understand better what is actually happening. Standing in front of the maps in the operations center, everything seems abstract, vague, and not very convincing. I have nothing of the Chief of Staff in me. I'm in complete possession of my faculties only when I'm directly confronted with events.

That particular Tuesday, for all General Riad's serenity —he was always in full command of himself, and no matter what was going on, he always found time to take a nap in a room set aside for him on the first floor at Headquarters— on that particular Tuesday, the turn of events seemed so critical that the atmosphere in the blockhouse became intolerable.

That is why I decided to go to the front, not out of love of battle—far from it!—but curiously enough, because the morale of my men was better, not to say more stimulating, than the atmosphere at Headquarters. It was far better for me too.

And yet, I will never forget the hallucinating sight of

that defeat. Roads clogged with trucks, jeeps, and all kinds of vehicles twisted, disemboweled, dented, still smoking, giving off that particular smell of metal and paint burned by exploding bombs—a stink that only powder can make. In the midst of this charnel house were men. In groups of 30 to 40, wounded, exhausted, they were trying to clear a path under the monstrous *coup de grâce* being dealt them by a horde of Israeli Mirages screaming in a cloudless blue sky seared with sun.

I identified the units each of the stricken men belonged to. I asked: "Where have you come from? What happened there?"

Each time, I heard the same request:

"Please, Sire, give us a few planes and we'll go back and fight!"

Planes!

When hostilities broke out yesterday, it was what we needed most. Today, not one of our planes is in condition to fight.

As I neared the front and the terrible spectacle of an army destroyed, a heartbreaking feeling of defeat came over me.

It was then that I ran into Colonel Rakan Anad, commander of the 40th tank brigade—far and away our best—and the Khaled Ibn El Walid brigade which had fought so valiantly at Jenin under the command of Colonel Awad Mohamed. I had worried about them.

Their tanks were drawn up on either side of the road and on this hot June afternoon, they smoked like monstrous horses exhausted from too long a ride. The overheated air stank of burning oil. The steel shells sweated grease and dust, like the men who drove them whose hanging chin straps revealed hastily knotted dirty bandages.

I could only thank these men for everything they had done under incredible conditions with never a thought of turning back.

I wanted very much to know what had happened to the 60th tank brigade under the command of my cousin Sherif Zeid Chaker. From the first day of the war, continued attacks by Israeli planes had almost entirely destroyed his brigade. He told me over the radio that he had only six tanks left and had withdrawn to the east bank. He then added:

"I am about to face some 80-odd Israeli tanks and armored vehicles coming toward the bridge on the main road to Amman."

Before I could answer, he went on:

"We are in control of the situation. We will do our best. Please, don't order us to retreat."

Many members of my family had gotten into uniform and several of them were wounded.

One of my cousins, Ali, the son of Prince Naif, was in this 60th tank brigade. He had been reported killed. I wanted to know if it was true. My family asked me to find out. At that moment, I came upon his unit. It was now or never. But I didn't dare. Before all those dead, growing in number from hour to hour, also with families, I felt I had no right to any prerogatives, not even that of asking after my cousin.

In Amman, which happily has not lost its sense of humor, they said: "The King has gone into battle taking his whole family with him." But the drama we were living through was not just one family's affair. It was for all Jordanians, for all the Arab nations!

I returned to Headquarters to get my bearings. They explained the situation to me as it evolved. I even considered the possibility of leaving with my personal guard to carry on the fight to the end.

At the close of the second day, I had no illusions left. Our cause was lost.

At 11:15 P.M., Nasser answered the message I had sent him that morning at 12:30 A.M. I learned for the first time that his air force was out of commission, and also that his situation on the ground was desperate. The U.A.R. President gave me a clear and accurate picture of his predicament which, up to then, we had been completely ignorant of.

"We have been purely and simply crushed by the enemy!" he summed up, and he advised me not to break off relations with London and Washington as he had.

Here is the text of Nasser's message to the Jordanian King:

My dear brother, King Hussein:

I have received your cable.

We find ourselves face to face with one of those critical moments that nations are sometimes called upon to endure. It demands courage beyond human capacity. We must face up to our responsibilities without fear of the consequences. We are fully aware of your difficult situation as at this very moment our front is crumbling too. Yesterday, our enemy's air force inflicted a mortal blow on us.* Since then, our

* This was the first and only reference to what had transpired the day before, to which no previous message from Cairo had made the slightest allusion. This means that the Jordanians had to wait 48 hours to learn what had really happened in Egypt at the start of the conflict, which determined the war's outcome.

land army has been stripped of all air support and forced to withstand the power of superior forces.

When the history books are written, your courage and tenacity will be remembered. They will not forget the heroic Jordanian people who went straight into battle without hesitation, and with no consideration other than honor and duty.

We have been the victims of aggression and we must face the situation without fear.

I think that our only choice now is to evacuate the west bank of the Jordan tonight, and hope that the Security Council will order a cease-fire.

The histories of nations are full of reverses, victories and defeats. We must hope that the choice we are making now—even though it seems bitter—will actually be our first step forward.

It is Allah's will—and maybe something good will come of it.

We trust in Allah and he will not desert us. Perhaps, thanks to him, the days ahead will bring us victory.

Finally, I want to tell you how much I appreciate your heroic behavior, your strong and gallant will, and the bravery shown by the Jordanian people and their army.

Salam Alaikoum Wa Rahmat Allah (Peace be with you and may Allah bless you).

Now follows King Hussein's response to Nasser's cable, sent at 2:30 in the morning of Wednesday, June 7:

I thank you from the bottom of my heart for your telegram, and wish to inform my brother that I have ordered all our troops on the west bank of the Jordan and all other fronts to hold onto their positions.

With God's help, may victory come to you as well as us.

A little later, I received another cable from Nasser which explained in detail all that had happened in Egypt:

Permit me to inform you of developments in the battle on the Egypt-Israel front.

The aggression was sudden and unexpected. From the first moment, its objective was to neutralize our air power. At the same time, the enemy attacked all our bases with many more planes than we had thought the Israeli air force possessed.

The High Command of our Armed Forces deduced that beyond a shadow of a doubt, the United States and Great Britain were aiding Israel.

The basis for this deduction was the intensity of the enemy's air offensive. We could not believe these vast resources belonged to Israel alone.

The result of all this was the destruction of our bases and our air power. From then on, our forces were unable to take effective action.

In spite of the heavy losses we inflicted on the opposing air force, it did seem as if the enemy had aircraft in reserve beyond the air cover America and Great Britain had established over Israel and which our side was lacking.

Even so, our forces in the Sinai engaged the enemy in violent battle and losses on both sides were very heavy.

I answered Nasser that we still had the option of a cease-fire. Whatever the means, we wanted an end to hostilities. We had no choice. I unwillingly resigned myself to this extremity, leaning on a kind of Oriental fatalism.

But when it came to accepting such a decision in the name of a fighting Arab nation, the task became intolerable. To let a people down at this point, after giving them so much hope, was to callously reward them with a disappointment they might not get over.

Leaders must take the responsibility for their mistakes. But to the citizens who have given them their confidence, what an irreparable deception!

It's true that I had foreseen what came to pass. I had given out warnings on many occasions. But was this enough? Could I in all decency take refuge in this easy excuse, hoping that eventually, "the people would understand our mistakes and rectify them themselves"?

At 11 P.M. Tuesday, June 6, an immediate and unconditional cease-fire was ordered by the United Nations. Our troops were still resisting in Hebron, Jerusalem, Ramallah and the area around Nablus—all on the west bank. The order came in the nick of time.

Unfortunately, General Riad had just directed the troops on the west bank to retreat to the east bank. Because we wanted to limit the casualties at all costs while holding on to as much land as possible, an immediate counterorder went out directing them to stay in their positions—which they had now held for 24 hours.

A few units had already moved back. They had to counterattack to regain what they had given up. On its side, Israel's cannons kept on hammering away. In fact, they intensified their offensive in order to win as much land as they could. In addition, Wednesday at 1:30 A.M., the brigade Imam Ali and the infantry brigade King Talal were ordered to hold their positions around Jerusalem to the last man.

At 2:30 A.M., we issued counterorders to these same units, instructing them to abide by the Security Council's cease-fire decision to the same degree as the Israelis. The same order was transmitted to the other units in other sections of the front.

At noon on Wednesday, Jerusalem fell after a desperate battle.*

Then it was Nablus's turn to capitulate. It had been bombed for 18 hours. Finally, the Israelis encircled Jericho and Hebron. Orders for a general retreat were issued to what remained of our army on Jordan's west bank, which henceforth was untenable.

The Israelis blew up the bridges, thus cutting off western Jordan from Trans-Jordan in order to establish their hold on the long-coveted west bank.

In the early hours of Thursday, June 8, the Jordanian government informed U Thant, the U.N. Secretary-General, that we accepted the Security Council's cease-fire.

The cease-fire did not really take hold until afternoon, as some of our men continued to fight independently to the very end.

For us, this Six Day so-called War was over, and Israel

---

* It was during that morning that General Dayan, the Israeli Defense Minister, refused to negotiate the cease-fire requested by Jordan with the remarks quoted earlier. Julien Besançon, a special correspondent for the Paris Radio station "Europe No. 1," filed a report describing the intensity of the Jordanians' defense of Arab Jerusalem: "On that Wednesday evening, June 7, I saw a Jordanian command car with a portrait of King Hussein on its radiator trying to break through the Mandelbaum Gate."

had stripped us of Jerusalem and the west bank of the Jordan.

Exhausted, his voice cracking with emotion, King Hussein addressed his people over Radio-Amman. From the start of the conflict, he had not slept or eaten. He was the only Arab leader who actually participated in the war; he was also the only one who addressed his people personally during the conflict.

"We have fought with heroism and honor. Some day the Arab nations will recognize the role Jordan played in the war.

"Our soldiers have defended every inch of our earth with their precious blood. It is not yet dry, but our country honors the stain. They were not afraid in the face of the total superiority of the enemy's air power which surprised and paralyzed the Egyptian air force (on which we had counted).

"Now, what's done is done. My heart breaks when I think of the loss of all our fallen soldiers. They were dearer to me than my own person.

"My brothers, I seem to belong to a family which, according to the will of Allah, must suffer and make sacrifices for its country without end. Our calamity is greater than any one could have imagined. But whatever its size, we must not let it weaken our resolve to regain what we have lost.

"If in the end you were not rewarded with glory, it was not because you lacked courage but because it was the will of Allah.

"May Allah now be with our people."

Chapter 14
An Inventory of Defeat

"The most important thing in this
story was to determine the truth . . ."

*What follows is an oft-interrupted conversation with King
Hussein in which we tried to clear up some points in what
had preceded.*

*How much aid did Jordan actually receive from its Arab
allies, only four of whom responded effectively when war
broke out—Egypt, Syria, Iraq and Saudi Arabia?*

Not much! We had no air cover from early on, so that
all our movements were paralyzed by constant attacks from
Israeli planes.

As for ammunition, food, etc., we had to make do with
what we had on hand.

*On this subject, we believe it is interesting to quote
extracts from the top-secret War Diary of the Jordanian
Chief of Staff, in which the activities of the allied Arab
forces on the Jordanian front are described hour by hour:*

SAUDI ARABIA: Incomplete brigade consisting of
three infantry battalions.

Thursday, June 1: The Saudi Arabians informed Jordanian Headquarters that their troops were arriving that
same day from Tabuk. We immediately dispatched
liaison officers to Mudawwara.

Tuesday, June 6: At 18:30, the Saudi Arabian troops (one

incomplete brigade comprising one infantry battalion and all its equipment) finally reached Mudawwara.

Wednesday, June 7: At 17:55, General Riad ordered them to proceed to El Quweira. The commander of the Saudi Arabian detachment answered that he would obey no orders to move until he had first received authorization from his headquarters in Tabuk.

Thursday, June 8: Arrival of a part of the 1st Saudi Arabian battalion in Ma'an in the late evening.

Friday, June 9: The remainder of the 1st battalion, the 2nd and the brigade staff followed. However, the Saudi Arabian detachment was not complete—with the 3d battalion—until Monday, June 12.

And so, the Saudi Arabian troops did not have an opportunity to take part in the war of June 1967.

UNITED ARAB REPUBLIC: 2 battalions of Egyptian commandos: the 33d and the 53d.

Saturday, June 3: Between 16 and 20 o'clock, eleven Egyptian planes delivered 2 battalions of commandos (the 33d and 53d) at the military airport in Amman.

The 33d was detached to serve with the Khaled Ibn El Walid brigade in the Jenin sector. The 53d joined the Hashemite brigade in the Ramallah sector.

Sunday, June 4: The rest of the Egyptian troops arrived from Cairo. The commander of the Egyptian detachment reconnoitered the terrain and picked out his objectives.

Monday, June 5: The Egyptian commandos were ordered to collaborate with the Jordanian commandos in the destruction of six enemy bases: the 33d was to move on the airports at Lydda, Ramla and Aqir; the 53d, on the airports at Kfar Cirkin, Herzliya and Ein Shamer.

To accomplish their mission, they were to cross the frontier at dusk.

The 33d succeeded, the 53d did not, except for the group headed toward Ein Shamer.

Tuesday, June 6: Those who managed to infiltrate enemy territory were not able to complete their missions. They had started too late. We asked them to return.

SYRIA: the 17th motorized brigade.

Tuesday, June 6: At 22 o'clock, Lt. Col. Adnan Tayyara, the former Syrian military attaché to the Syrian Ambassador in Jordan, en route to Amman, informed the border authorities that the 17th motorized infantry brigade would be arriving within the hour.

Wednesday, June 7: 2 A.M. The 17th brigade has not yet arrived.

2:15: General Riad contacted the War Room in Damascus and asked to be reinforced by another tank brigade as soon as possible. At the same time, he informed Damascus that the 17th brigade had still not arrived.

11:00: The 17th brigade has not yet reached Ramtha, the first post on the Syrian-Jordan border.

20:20: Forward elements of the 17th brigade were finally sighted. The Syrian commander was ordered to occupy defensive positions in the Wadi Shu'eb axis as soon as he had his full complement of men, so as to permit the Jordanian forces to regroup.

Thursday, June 8: The Syrian commander spent the day

studying his new positions with his officers before proceeding to occupy them.

20:00: The 17th battalion was still at its initial concentration point at Buke'a.

22:00: The Jordanian liaison officer attached to the 17th brigade reported to General Riad that the brigade's commander refused to take possession of the designated positions, and that he asked for another delay until tomorrow. He said that he wanted his company commanders to make a more detailed survey of the area.

General Riad tried in vain to convince the Syrian commander to execute his maneuver that same night.

Friday, June 9: General Riad informed the Syrian commander that he could return to Syria with his troops at the close of day.

The 17th brigade retired as directed.

It did not participate in any action.

Even so, we noted, the Syrians seemed to want war. The head of the Syrian government, Dr. Youseff Zouein, had even said in Cairo: "The time for words is over. The time for war has come . . ." Was this just bravado, or was it the verbal poker game typical of certain Orientals?

The King replied:

Only time will answer many of these questions. What I do know is this: on the 5th of June, the Syrian air force was not ready to fight. The Israelis were smart to hold back only 12 planes for their own defense while sending the greater part of their air power on its first offensive against the Egyptian bases. Especially since there proved to be no air cover over the U.A.R.

On Saturday the 3rd and Sunday the 4th of June, the Egyptian air force was in the air in a state of constant alert. Then on Monday the 5th, nothing. Why?

The truth is that Marshal Abdel Hakim Amer, Vice-President of the United Arab Republic and Commander in Chief of its armed forces, was to leave for a tour of inspection of the Sinai front that day, together with General Mahmoud Sidki, Commander in Chief of the Egyptian air force, and several officers on the Egyptian General Staff. Therefore, the order had gone out that no planes were to be fired on that morning.

The attitude of the Egyptian air force during the conflict has often been argued. It's my view that it was following perfectly justifiable orders within a fixed strategy. Its failure was due to a most unfortunate set of circumstances.

King Hussein is not alone in this opinion. The French weekly, Paris Match, *has reported that General Mordekai Hodd, Commander of the Israeli air force, had proposed to go to Cairo to defend General Sidki when he was condemned to 15 years' imprisonment for professional malfeasance in the defeat of June 5.*

In the article, Hodd said:

I do not know General Sidki personally. He was and remains my enemy. But the proceedings of the court-martial in Cairo revolt me.

On that morning of June 5, at 4 o'clock, Sidki did exactly what he had to do. He sent a patrol of 12 Egyptian planes to the Israeli border. Day was breaking over Sinai.

From 4:15 to 7 in the morning, three other patrols of 12 Migs each were flying every half hour over the Mediterranean and the Suez Canal. Sidki had no way of knowing that at that same moment, 7 A.M. (8 o'clock Egyptian time), I had decided to attack his bases in broad daylight.

I remember very well the anxiety I felt that morning at 7:30. Our planes were nearing the Egyptian coastline. Suddenly our radar showed the silhouette of an Illyushin 14 over the Suez Canal flying toward Sinai. It was the plane carrying Marshal Amer and General Sidki.

It was impossible to alert our pilots because they were flying very low and had their radios off in order to go unnoticed. The Illyushin 14 could easily discover our air fleet and give the alarm to the Egyptian air force.

Was it Sidki's fault if he was on a tour of inspection with Marshal Amer at the moment of our attack? He had no way of knowing the day and hour of the attack. Their intelligence had provided them with nothing concerning Israel's plans. Nor had his adviser, the Soviet general, anticipated anything.

The operational plans of the Chief of Staff of the Egyptian air force, which we found after the conquest of Sinai, were perfect in every respect. It would have cost us much if Sidki had been able to execute them.

What General Hodd said was confirmed by Mohamed Hassanein Heykal, editor in chief of the Egyptian daily, Al Ahram, who is known in Cairo to be Nasser's trusted friend. Mr. Heykal reported:

On that Monday, June 5, the presence in Egyptian skies of the plane carrying Marshal Abdel Hakim Amer [the regime's No. 2 man who apparently "committed suicide" after the June defeat], Lt. Gen. Mahmoud Sidki and the top officers of the Egyptian General Staff, paralyzed all action from the Egyptian antiaircraft batteries equipped with ground air missiles, which were the latest Soviet model.

The plane carrying the military "brain trust" of the United Arab Republic was following the route towards the Thamad base on the Sinai front and, because of the Israeli air offensive, it had to stay in the air for an hour and a half before it was able to return and land at the international airport in Cairo.

And what about Shukairy? How did he conduct himself during the conflict?

King Hussein replied:

Shukairy left Amman for Jerusalem on Saturday June 3 —still wearing his Mao-style uniform—in order to hold a press conference in which he made one of those thundering declarations so useful to Israeli propaganda.

On Monday the 5th, toward noon, he arrived at Riad's headquarters in Amman. But this time he was in civilian clothes. He stayed with us the whole afternoon and seemed full of confidence. The day after, on Tuesday the 6th, he suddenly left for Syria. He wanted to ask Damascus to give us a little more help than it had up to now.* Anyway, this subject does not deserve any further comment on my part.

The King was asked: What part did the Iraqi troops and the Palestinian detachment play in the war?

The Palestinian battalion acted jointly with the Iraqi forces to which it was attached. But actually, they were put out of commission very early.

I had several telephone contacts with Aref, the President of Iraq, during those tragic days. I will never forget the way

---

* King Hussein's version of Shukairy's departure is not accepted by well-informed Jordanians and foreigners. In Amman, it was generally said that "Shukairy simply wished to escape the war's danger zones. It was this that explained his successive flights—which were more than just departures—from Jerusalem, then Amman, then Damascus, as the front grew nearer."

Iraq came to our aid, or the condition of the Iraqi troops when they arrived in the Jordan valley, ignoring the enormous losses they had suffered.

They had only just left the north of Iraq where they had been trying to put down a Kurd rebellion, when they had to go straight to Jordan. The 8th Iraqi motorized brigade arrived in the Mafraq zone at midnight, Monday, June 5. On the move during the entire war, it was continually harassed by enemy planes. The greater part of its equipment was destroyed. In spite of this, the Iraqi soldiers kept up their dogged advance on the positions they'd been assigned, down to their last vehicle. They felt it their duty to help us at whatever the cost.

At 5 P.M. on Tuesday, the 6th, Iraq sent us its 1st infantry brigade as reinforcements, then its 27th infantry brigade and its 6th tank brigade.

The Iraqi drivers did not sleep for an entire week. Even though they were exhausted, they shuttled between Baghdad and the Jordan valley bringing tanks to the front. I admired them. All those days without rest, without food. What quality! They did everything that was humanly possible.

After that ordeal, I am happy that our relations with Iraq have been revived.

How did your lines of communications function during the war?

Our radio connections were very bad. The Israelis intercepted them often, both in the air and on the ground. And the constant bombing of our troops was an added aggravation.

What role did Jordanian and Arab intelligence play? Was there good collaboration during the conflict?

Israeli intelligence was the most efficient in the entire Middle East. They had been preparing this operation for years. The two pilots we took prisoner told us that they'd been training for a year and a half on models that were exact replicas of the objectives they each would have to attack.

As far as we Jordanians are concerned, we had never done any air reconnaissance over Israel. We can't say as much for them.

As for the Arabs' intelligence, it underestimated Israel's power. And there was no collaboration during the conflict. We had never had occasion to cooperate in the past, and that was also a handicap.

You were present at the decisions made by General Riad. What do you think of him?

It's quite true that I was present at all Riad's decisions. I even helped with some of them. Riad wanted my approval of those he considered most important.

The most painful decision for me was to accept General Riad's proposal to withdraw our troops to the east bank of the Jordan. It was a hard choice because we were abandoning our own people on the west bank and in Jerusalem.

As for Riad himself, he is a professional soldier and a capable officer. His background was excellent.

While we're on that subject, I well remember that Tuesday evening, June 6, when we were waiting together for the Syrian reinforcements. A Syrian officer had been sent on ahead and arrived at Headquarters to inquire about the situation in general, and to prepare for liaison between the Syrian troops and our own.

As we gave him the full story of that critical evening, he

listened placidly with no reaction. When we finished briefing him, he said with complete indifference:

"In other words, the west bank of the Jordan is lost?"

I must admit that for the first time since the Israeli offensive began, I felt the blood rush to my head. How could he be so unmoved? How could he be so oblivious to the facts?

Riad indicated the advance posts we wished the Syrians to occupy so that we ourselves could regroup. For all the endless hemming and hawing, the Syrian detachment never did accomplish its mission and failed to participate in a single operation.

On the one hand, we had the Israelis to fight; on the other, the frustration of getting anything done. It was so bad that one day Riad said:

"My hardest job has been to play U Thant between the Syrians and you!"

We nicknamed him U Thant from then on.

In Riad's view, the worst errors committed during the war were attributable to Arab political problems. They impeded our armed forces far more than the Israelis.

I am in complete agreement with him.

Considering the peculiar character of the two-day battle in Jordan which Riad had to wage, knowing neither the terrain nor the capacities of the men under his command, while at the mercy of the fantastic misinformation regarding the situation on the various allied fronts, he could not have done better.

When hostilities were over, Riad stayed in Jordan for a few days to await the arrival of the Syrian forces and to coordinate them with the Iraqi forces.

Before returning to Cairo, he came to say good-by. It

was afternoon in my new offices in the palace which replaced those machine-gunned by the Israelis.

I thanked him for his help, in spite of everything that had happened:

"You did your best," I said to ease his confusion.

He told me how proud he was of the way our troops had behaved. He made a few more remarks, including the perfectly justifiable criticism about Arab politics being responsible for our debacle.

He was as unhappy as we were over the way the battle had ended in Jerusalem and elsewhere.

A fraternity of arms united us. All of us who worked with him consider him a friend.

Were you tempted to sanction some of your errors by using court-martial, as the Egyptians did with some of their superior officers?

No. I believe everyone acted to the best of his capacities, faculties and possibilities.

Some did far more than that.

Others could not have done more.

And the limitations of others made it useless to hope for more.

Moreover, I never felt any hostility or bitterness in my dealings with my officers and soldiers. We analyzed the entire operation. Every decision taken during the war and its aftermath has been carefully studied.

Of course I couldn't help being deeply affected by the idea that 15 years of work, of hard labor—for me as well as those who worked with me—had come to a head in the dramatic situation before us. I've asked myself several times since if I was right in certain decisions. It's a challenge you must find the courage to face.

As a result of the June defeat, our geographic and strategic situation was altered by the loss of the west bank and of our military potential. So we came to the conclusion that we had to revise our politics of defense and totally reorganize our means of defense in order to avoid repeating the mistakes we made during that so-called war.

Yes, that's what I said: "THAT SO-CALLED WAR WITH ISRAEL!"

I didn't fight under real war conditions. I never declared war on Israel and I never made war with Israel. Naturally, I responded to each of Israel's acts of aggression, in 1956, in 1967, and still more recently, in 1968.

A state of war has existed in the Middle East since 1948. During this period we have had an armistice. Not peace. Nor have the conditions of this armistice been easy; more often than not, they have been ruptured by the Israelis.

As for peace, it is still far off.

Until a just solution is found, there can be no question of peace.

Today, we continue to hold fast and we fight with what we have left. But thanks to our military reorganization, the results are entirely different.

Recently, on March 21, 1968, nine months after the June defeat, the Israelis conducted a raid against Shuna and Karameh, on the east side of the Jordan. But our response transformed a simple "police action" into a real military engagement; the aggressors suffered entirely unexpected losses despite the continuous air cover for their many tanks and their truck- and helicopter-borne troops.

We Jordanians have learned our lesson on how to conduct a limited action with a reduced air force, and what air cover to expect from our allies.

One of our basic mistakes in the June conflict was not tailoring our operations to our resources and leaving aside all help from the outside. We held to the principle of protecting Arab strategic interests in general while reducing our own to a secondary level.

As a result, since we had counted on help from allies who, for one reason or another, failed to honor their agreements, we were forced as the operation ran its course to improvise with the means we had available at the moment.

Most of the time, our means turned out to be less than we had counted on and insufficient for our needs to oppose the enemy's tactics.

In a way, Israel imposed its style of combat on us through the cohesion of its strategy, while we had to consider the logistic interests of our several allies. For example, that maneuver of the 40th and 60th tank brigades: it was dictated by General Riad's desire to relieve the Egyptian troops in the south who were supposed to be joining up with our own, and also by the Syrian failure in the north which deprived us of essential support if we were to present a common front against the Israeli offensive.

These factors caused much confusion in our camp.

Since the June 1967 defeat, have you rebuilt your military power?

Iraq has furnished us a few tanks to replace some of those we lost. But we still feel the repercussions of the war. In the face of continued skirmishes, we try to hold on with what we have.

Recently, the Americans decided to rearm us by mutual agreement.

In the meantime, we have been borrowing equipment from our neighbors, but not in large quantities, and have

managed to buy a few Hawker Hunters. But it will take
time to rebuild our air force. Actually, it is not a question
of whether we are able to buy more planes. You can always get military matériel. That's not the problem. It's all
in knowing how to get the money for these purchases.

We hope to find a solution to this problem during the
course of new Arab meetings, for we Jordanians bore the
war's heaviest burden and suffered the most from the defeat.

*On a more personal level: What was your relationship
with your family during the June conflict?*

I made one or two brief telephone calls to my family,
and one quick trip to my house—in the hills on the edge of
Amman—to make sure everything was all right. My wife,
Princess Muna, knew exactly how to behave under the
circumstances. She did not panic or lose her head. She remained very calm, in full control, very brave and clear-
headed.

Our two little boys, Abdullah [five years old] and Faisal
[three and a half], had a marvelous time, especially the
younger one who has a passion for airplanes. Whenever
they could steal away, they rushed to the terrace to watch
the Israeli planes thundering by. They were thrilled by
the noise they made, because the bombing was not very
far from us. They were too young to realize the significance of what was happening.

*And then the King of Jordan returned to the subject
nearest his heart, his army.*

It was the afternoon of the cease-fire. I had gone down
into the valley * to find out what was left of our troops,
and especially the 60th tank brigade.

* The Jordan valley.

From the start of hostilities, I had had no time to wash, change my clothes or even sleep. I had stopped thinking about it. When I wasn't at Headquarters in Amman, I was at the front, and when I left the front, it was to return to Headquarters. From time to time, I nibbled a sandwich which I seldom finished, although I drank liters of tea and smoked one cigarette after another. It reached the point where I couldn't tell the difference between the filter Chesterfields I usually smoked and any other brand that came to hand.

And so, when I arrived that afternoon at advance Headquarters at the front near the Jordan River, where I was expected, I had an extraordinary experience. There I was with several days' beard and a dirty uniform, and the officers who greeted me were correctly dressed and clean-shaven, even though they had been fighting without letup under intolerable conditions. In spite of it, they had made an effort to spruce up. I felt most uncomfortable and I have to admit that I was a little ashamed of my slovenliness.

During the conflict, did you ever wish you were in your men's place rather than in your own?

Oh yes! Often! I had an enormous feeling of relief when I could leave the blockhouse at headquarters and see what was happening for myself. It's not in my temperament to experience only in theory what my men are actually going through.

Chapter 15
The War's Aftermath

*"I realized that our most important task
was to devise a political strategy more
effective than our military one had been."*

The King continues:

So far as I personally was concerned, the most difficult period in this infernal cycle came between the June defeat and the summit conference of the Arab countries in Khartoum from August 29 to September 1, 1967. This ill-starred period affected both my physical and moral health. I came out of it desperately tired and discouraged. It was all too hard, too painful.

Fortified by this new experience, I had traveled over the Arab world, and the rest of the world as well, trying to explain what had really happened in the part of the world called the Middle East.

We have a challenge to meet: we must combat the general lack of understanding about the Israeli-Arab conflict.

At the beginning of this century, the Israelis had had a definite objective: they wanted to get to this area and install themselves in Palestine. They were particularly clever at influencing world opinion to accept their aspirations.

As viewed by the world, the Arabs give the impression of being irresponsible and unstable. But this judgment is superficial and mistaken when you consider our internal

113

problems. What we really want is to contribute to the progress of civilization while regaining our rightful place in history and in the concert of nations.

It was with this in mind that I went before the United Nations and visited the heads of the great powers.

Before going to the U.N. where, on June 27, I was to address the delegates as spokesman for the Arab cause, I realized that our most important task was to devise a political strategy more effective than our military one had been. That was why I was so eager for a summit conference of the Arab countries. But I couldn't bring it off in time; it didn't take place until the end of August, at Khartoum, almost three months after our defeat.

I also made a tour of those world leaders who were capable of playing a role in the Arab drama.

I first went to see the President of the United States, Mr. L. B. Johnson. He was understanding, attentive to my proposals, but a little bitter—very bitter, in fact—about the attitude of certain Arabs toward the United States, particularly Egypt.

He was equally critical of Israel's actions, since it had assured him it would not take the military initiative.

He wanted to contribute as far as he was able to the search for some kind of peaceful solution to the problem.

In London, the head of the British government, Mr. Harold Wilson, and his Foreign Minister, Mr. [George] Brown, were also very friendly and well informed about the situation. In spite of the open hostility shown us by English public opinion—toward me, my country and Arabs in general—we arrived at a mutual understanding.

In Paris, President Charles de Gaulle was extremely understanding, thanks to his thorough knowledge of the

problem and its many aspects. His attitude of concern and
his friendliness toward us touched me a great deal. I remember his words: "If Israel has the right to live in peace
and security, Jordan certainly has earned the same right!"

As I left de Gaulle, I felt reassured and more cheerful.
I thanked him in the name of the entire Arab world and
expressed the admiration we all felt for him.

De Gaulle considered that the great powers had an obli-
gation to help us find a just solution and that aggression
should not pay.

A little later, on October 2, I went to Moscow where I
met with President Podgorny and his Prime Minister, Mr.
Kosygin. I was warmly received. It was my first visit to the
Soviet Union.

After thanking the Russians for their steadfast support
of the Arab world, I tried to dispel the misunderstandings
that had strained relations between Moscow and Amman.

The Soviet leaders showed an extensive knowledge of
our problem and assured us of their continued support.

Wherever I went, one point was made abundantly clear:
in spite of the tragic turn in the Palestinian problem,
world opinion was convinced that ISRAEL IS IN THIS
PART OF THE WORLD TO STAY.

It was there for all to see. But at the same time, I sensed
the definite desire to help us define our position in relation
to the fact of Israel, and to make certain that peace would
not give Israel the right to any form of territorial expansion. They were also anxious to help us establish a just and
lasting peace and mitigate the after-effects of the June war.

*What about Nasser? What do you think of him? When
did you see him again after the June debacle?*

I think of Nasser as a partner, an associate, a friend.

Soon after the June disaster, I spent a night in Cairo in order to see him before I went before the United Nations. He was very cordial. Already, during the course of the June war, Nasser's attitude toward Jordan and myself had changed completely. Perhaps he learned the truth about us, as we did about him.

As a result of our several meetings, he showed himself to be most reasonable and convincing in his moderation. His point of view turned out to be quite similar to mine.

He had followed the same process of reappraisal we had: he had recognized his weaknesses, where he had committed his mistakes, and he was trying to rebuild on a more stable and realistic base. Of course, his losses in June had been enormous.

We wanted to make common cause in the diplomatic battle we were to wage and to bring about Arab unanimity in the search for a viable solution. We agreed on this at the time of the summit conference in Khartoum; it holds true today.

During the U.N. General Assembly session, it appeared for a while that, thanks to the cooperative efforts of the United States and the Soviet Union, we might get a more favorable resolution than the one the Security Council had offered. This was sabotaged by Arab extremists. We had tried very hard to work together with the Americans. But because of the way some of us behaved, the Americans wound up saying:

"What are we to do? You act against us when we are trying to help!"

The same with the Russians, who asked us:

"What is it you Arabs really want?"

At all costs, we had to define what exactly we Arabs

really wanted. I had been asked this over and over again. Before I returned to Europe and the United States at the end of 1967 to pursue my battle for peace, I went back to see Nasser to try to work out an "Arab position."

It was September 30, 1967, a few weeks after the Khartoum Arab summit conference where the U.A.R. and Jordan had arrived at a common political program which the other Arab nations had agreed to support.

I have an unforgettable memory of that visit with Nasser, or rather, of my arrival in Cairo.

I had left Amman in the morning. At 11 A.M., we were 100 kilometers from Cairo. As usual, I was at the controls. I asked the tower in Cairo for permission to land. The man in charge answered:

"The airport is shut down because of a sand storm."

"Can we land in Alexandria?" I asked.

"That's closed too."

"What about Beirut?"

"The weather is closing in there too."

"What are the other possibilities?"

"Cyprus."

I reported this to the other men in the cabin.

One of them said, "Better not set down in Cyprus. That would be open to all kinds of interpretations."

Everybody laughed.

I then asked the tower:

"Has no plane landed in Cairo this morning?"

The answer left me aghast:

"I haven't the faintest idea."

I checked my fuel and the chief pilot said:

"We can just make Beirut or Cyprus, Sire, but we

haven't enough to go back to Amman. The weather is probably about to close that airport too."

"Couldn't we try to come down here?" I asked.

"We can try, but only once," the chief pilot said. "If we don't make it, we won't have enough fuel to do anything else."

The runways at the Cairo airport were edged with hills of sand. I decided to approach the runway at the lowest possible altitude, using navigation instruments, and started to make the descent. I couldn't see a thing. I dropped another 200 meters. I could vaguely make out the end of the runway; then I landed.

We were no sooner down than we rushed from the plane to the shelter of the air terminal. What a relief!

And so I met Nasser, and we decided together on the five points defining the "Arab position":

1. We would be willing to recognize everyone's right to live in peace and security in the area, including Israel's.

2. We agreed to bring an end to the state of belligerency and the war.

3. We agreed to open the international waterways, including the Suez Canal, to all nations.

The first two provisions required reciprocal action from the Israelis, providing:

4. That the Israelis withdraw from all the territories occupied during the June 1967 conflict;

5. That a real solution is found for the living symbol of our continual state of war—the refugees: that they would be given the right to return to their land, or adequate compensation in accordance with the earliest resolutions of the United Nations.

Some of these points were already in the Soviet-U.S.

resolution, which was abandoned because of the Arab extremists' reactions.

Immediately after leaving Nasser I went to Algiers. There it was agreed that we should try what we proposed and that Algeria would not interfere. But they were skeptical.

It was following these efforts that Gunnar Jarring set off on his peace mission, the result of a unanimous resolution passed by the Security Council in November '67.

The U.N. resolution and the five points Nasser and I worked out found a mixed reception in the Arab world. Some thought that even if we achieved all this, we would still be far from a satisfactory solution. Others didn't believe in the possibility of a just and peaceful solution, but agreed to let us try.

In the end, we accepted the Security Council resolution and indicated our desire to see it applied.* Israel had reservations about it and refused to accept it. That is why Dr. Jarring's mission is so slow and precarious in its unfolding.

Since Arab unanimity is so hard to come by, what do you think of the possibility of a separate peace between Jordan and Israel to solve the Palestinian problem?

No. That is neither possible nor sensible. The quarrel must be resolved all of a piece and not in fragments.

Everything must be coordinated. I've done everything in my power to achieve this.

Israel must contribute to a solution of the Palestinian problem as a whole so that the peace will be definitive. And now is the time to do it. A peace between Jordan and Israel, or Palestine and Israel is simply useless.

We have shown that we are ready to go a long way to-

---

* Not all Arab countries did.

ward its realization, and to accept the challenge of building a better future for this region as an indivisible whole.

Now it's Israel's turn. It's up to them, the victors, to
prove by actions that they really mean to live in peace with
the Arabs and be accepted in this world on which they
have encrusted themselves like a scab.

Chapter 16
And Now . . .

*"Israel is in this part
of the world to stay."*

King Hussein continues:

I am nearing the end.

The Jarring mission is our first and last chance to establish peace with Israel. A durable peace. And to be durable, it must be just. At the moment, everything is suspended because of Israel. According to whether Jarring succeeds or fails, it will or won't be the end to this chance for peace.

Yes. The Jarring mission is our last chance.

Time is running out. I am afraid of the feeling of pessimism that may submerge the Arab world: "We cannot succeed with a political solution."

Unless Jarring can show definite progress, this part of the world is in danger of being dragged into a merciless struggle. And despite some probable Israeli victories, it will be a long war ending with the defeat of Israel, and therefore, a threat to world peace.

And, the King was asked, what about Jerusalem?

As far as Jerusalem is concerned, it is not a question of our giving up our rights. They are not our rights alone, but those of all Moslems. This is no longer a Jordanian problem, but a Moslem problem, an Arab and a Christian problem.

Should peace come, there would no longer be a problem

for believers and their religious observances. But we cannot give up our rights to Jerusalem, for they go back more than a thousand years.

Jerusalem is a religious problem. You mustn't forget that to Moslems the Holy City is the second place of pilgrimage after Mecca. It's interesting to remember how Jerusalem became sacred to Moslems.

Mount Scopus, where the Mosque of Omar was built in Jerusalem, is called in Arabic "Gabal Al Mukhabbar."

In the seventh century when Jerusalem was seized by the Arabs, the Greek Orthodox patriarch was all-powerful. He agreed to open the gates of the city to the conquerors, but refused to give the keys to the commander of the Arab armies.

"I will give them only to the Caliph himself," he said.

So Omar Ibn El Katab, the second Caliph in Mecca, had to come to Jerusalem. He made the trip with one servant because he was poor, and saddled only one camel for the two of them. Omar and his servant took turns riding the beast. When they reached Jerusalem, it was the servant's turn in the saddle; Omar followed behind on foot. And so they arrived at Mount Scopus.

"Allah Akbar!" ("God is all powerful!") Omar repeated twice as he prostrated himself.

From that day on, Mount Scopus became the Moslems' "Gabal Al Mukhabbar," or "The mountain of he who said 'God is all powerful.' "

Worn out by the trip, on foot while his servant sat enthroned on the camel, the Caliph in his humble garments didn't look the part. The patriarch couldn't recognize the Caliph Omar in this miserable traveler. But after a long discussion, he accepted the evidence and gave the Caliph the keys to Jerusalem, which he then invited him to visit.

At noon—the Moslem hour of prayer—Omar found himself with the patriarch in the Church of the Holy Sepulchre. He stopped and asked the Greek Orthodox patriarch:

"May I go to pray in the gardens over there?"

"You say we believe in the same God," the patriarch said. "Why do you refuse to pray in our church?"

"I refuse to pray here because I am afraid lest one day the Moslems in the city learn where I prayed. They will then want to build a mosque here where your church stands."

One hundred and fifty years later, the Moslems did build the Mosque of Omar in the gardens next to the Holy Sepulchre, exactly where the Caliph had said his prayers.

I think this story demonstrates the tolerance that Islam has always shown to other religious communities.

If Israel insists on clinging to Jerusalem, that will be reason enough for Arabs and all Moslems to make certain that the Jews withdraw behind their lines.

You mustn't forget that David and Solomon's political state lasted only seventy years, and the Crusaders' less than a century.

Israel would do well to reread its history.

As we have seen, King Hussein speaks as if he were the sole master of his country's fate. However, he must also take into account the differences in his entourage which reflect other aspects of Jordanian opinion.

For this reason, it is interesting to hear what certain

other people highly placed in Jordanian circles have to say about the Palestinian question.

In particular:

Wasfi al Tall, the ex-Prime Minister of Jordan, who disapproved of Nasser;

Yehia Hammoude, Shukairy's successor as head of the Palestine Liberation Organization which includes most of the Arab extremists dedicated to the idea of wiping Israel off the map;

And the Palestinian Commandos, the combat groups of refugees whose only goal is to reclaim their country.

Chapter 17
Wasfi al Tall

"We could easily have avoided this premature war."

Wasfi al Tall speaks:

After my resignation,* the political currents in Jordan unfortunately moved toward a *rapprochement* with Nasser. By currents, I mean a mixture—bits and pieces of everything: the new group around the King, political pressures, popular emotion, etc., and even certain maneuvers by the United States.

I was unhappy with the turn of events. I had a premonition of what would happen. I warned everybody, but no one would listen.

I didn't think we were ready for war. We had decided to reinforce ourselves, to try to protect the armistice line and to avoid giving Israel an excuse to drag us into a premature war. That was why we didn't want to retaliate after Es Samu. And why we tried to prevent commandos from provoking incidents along the armistice line. All this was in order to achieve a position of strength so that we could some day reclaim our rights by whatever means necessary—military, economic or political.

This was our political line, and also that of all the other

* The Prime Minister left the government when a new Parliament was formed during the crisis following the Israeli police action at Es Samu in November 1966.

Arabs: we were all anxious not to give Israel the slightest excuse for starting a war when it did not suit us. And ever since the first Arab summit meeting, our common political aim—for what it was worth—had been not to encourage commando activity.

We could easily have avoided this premature war. Of course, we hardly expected such a devastating defeat. But with the information we had, we didn't believe in the possibility of victory either.

Nasser was bluffing. He wanted to push things to the limit, to poke around in the crack, but not to the point of rupture. He overestimated his abilities as a politician.

The Syrians thought they were immune from Israeli attack: they knew that it would be Jordan (for whom they had no love) and Egypt (whom they didn't like as much as people were led to believe) who would have to bear the brunt of the war. Actually, they never did and still don't want to fight.

Certainly, there was a general plan for Arab defense, but in theory only, not in fact. Even during the June war, the plan was not applied, for basically, no Arab really believed that war was coming, although everything they saw made them fear it.

Already in 1956, we had a unified command involving Syria, Egypt, Saudi Arabia and us. The Commander in Chief was the same Egyptian, Marshal Abdel Hakim Amer, who is thought to have "committed suicide" after the June defeat. Our Prime Minister in Amman was Soliman Naboulsi, who headed a pro-Nasser cabinet made up of Socialists, Baathists and Communists. But when Egypt was attacked, these same cabinet members thought twice about getting involved. Nasser expected them to intervene. But here, as in Syria, they launched into interminable discussions on what attitude to adopt. By the time they had finished, the Egyptian army was defeated.

To save face, Nasser cabled King Hussein, who was doing his best to hurry the cabinet along, asking him not to intervene because the British-French participation made it hopeless.

We Jordanians take the Palestinian question very seriously. It affects us more than Egyptians, Syrians, Iraqis, or any other Arab nation. That is why it's so convenient for us to be made the scapegoat. We were prodded into joining the others in the 1967 war not by the fear of public opinion or a desire to be in on the spoils, but by our honor, which demanded that we observe our mutual defense agreements.

It should be noted that Jordan had for a long time been organizing its defense with what means it had. During normal times, the army disposed along the armistice line had permanent orders to prevent any Israeli incursions, without referring decisions to a higher level. We certainly would have been better off had we used our usual defense methods rather than waiting on General Riad's decisions as to whether it should be done this way or that.

Riad made some very serious mistakes.

The first was to believe Egypt's statement: "we have crushed the enemy air force and are crossing the Israeli frontier." We didn't have a single Jordanian liaison officer in Egypt! It's incredible! Thus we were at the mercy of whatever false information Egypt decided to give out.

On the first day of the battle, Riad was totally ignorant of what had actually happened to the U.A.R. air force until late in the afternoon or evening—I no longer remember which—when a telegram from Cairo admitted the real facts. We were all there with him in the neon-lit block-house at General Headquarters, and with no windows to the outside, we had lost all sense of time.

It was Riad who made the monumental error of shifting the 40th and 60th tank brigades over the objections of everyone involved.

That was his second big mistake.

Even if our information on the destruction of the Israeli air force had been accurate, in no way did it justify Riad's decision to shift the tank brigades. Strategically, it was non-sense. Moreover, because the Jordanians' tanks did not know there would be no allied air cover and wanted to execute the order as fast as possible, they made their moves fully exposed. Thus they were at the mercy of the enemy air force whose unexpected size convinced everyone that there had been Anglo-American intervention. I never be-lieved it for a moment!

There is one consolation we can draw from this catas-trophe: our officers objected to every one of Riad's orders, even though they were obliged to obey.

Riad had a general staff made up of four or five Egyp-tian high officers and they made all the decisions. Eti-quette in the operations center permitted few suggestions or counter-suggestions. The Jordanian Brigadier, Atef Majali [now dead], who was Riad's assistant in the United Arab Command, objected strongly to some of his decisions, but Riad was a stubborn man. The same applied to the divisions and brigades on the west bank where most of Riad's orders were opposed by the officers involved. They called on Atef Majali to persuade Riad that various orders were unwise and to plead their case before the Egyptian general. But Riad wouldn't listen, and in the end, what he decided was done.

Riad was obstinate, not so much from a desire to impose his authority as out of disinterest: he didn't much care. Or perhaps his confidence in Egypt's omnipotent military power made him detached. Or perhaps it was his incompetence, which could also make for a certain detachment.

In any event, as with a surgical operation, we were only spectators. You can't have more than one captain on a ship. Therefore, there was no other attitude to take.

Riad looks a little like me. He is big, dark-skinned, but with no mustache. He wears glasses and smokes American cigarettes. Riad is a lively and intelligent man but his relaxed manner is actually a form of paralysis. For all the pontifications intended to impress us with his superior knowledge, we discovered that he was not equal to the situation. On paper, his credentials were splendid: attendance at the British military college, then various tours of duty in the United States, the Soviet Union and France. He had been Chief of Staff of the United Arab Command since 1964. Consequently, it was his duty to know the army he was commanding and the terrain on which it would have to maneuver. He had visited Jordan several times for this purpose. So he had no excuse.

This is Israel's last chance to withdraw to its old armistice line with Jordan. If it doesn't do it now, the present state of hostilities will prevail. Commando operations will automatically multiply. The Israelis will consider themselves obliged to respond as they did in Shuna and Karameh on March 21, 1968. That cost them a lot. They will have to stay mobilized for an indefinite period. And if they continue to attack Jordan, the Arabs will eventually agree to help her and give her the air cover she needs.

If this does happen, time will be on our side and not theirs. The efforts of all the Arab nations will be placed at Jordan's disposal and Jordan will become the springboard for Arab resistance.

Jordan cannot act separately in peace negotiations, if for no other reason than conviction and principle.

The commandos are a perfectly natural and spontaneous phenomenon. Their ties with the Egyptians and Syrians in no way detract from their desire for a national identity.

If the Israelis withdrew to the prewar armistice line, peace discussions could then be based on a true realization of the partition drawn up by the United Nations in 1947. (Authors' note: In other words, Israel would give up a part of the Negev, western Galilee, and so on. This hardly corresponds to the five points in the "Arab position" drawn up by Nasser and King Hussein.)

Chapter 18
Yehia Hammoude
(Shukairy's successor)

"Zionism is an imperialist and colonial transplant."

Yehia Hammoude speaks:

We know that the West will never be on our side. The Zionist cause is political. The Zionist movement was grafted onto the heart of the Arab world and its activities are encouraged for imperialist ends. This is when everything started.

Zionism is an imperialist and colonial transplant. The West is interested in the exploitation of our oil, etc. I'm speaking of the Western governments and not their people, for the people as a whole are not responsible for these conditions. We are the victims of politicians and businessmen. Our war is therefore a war of liberation. We must liberate our land from colonialism! It's like the Algerian war. But colonialism in our case is camouflaged behind Jewish allegations based on historical and spiritual pretexts. That is their justification for this colonial operation.

The aggression against our land began in 1917 with the Balfour Declaration. In 1917, Palestine had 750,000 inhabitants of whom only 50,000 were Jews. The remainder were Moslems and Christians. But they were all Arabs. The Jewish minority lived in peace, particularly in Jerusalem. In most of the Palestinian towns, there was a Jewish quarter.

There were also a few small Jewish colonies. The ε represented less than half of one per cent of the total land surface.

The struggle began in 1917 with uprisings against the Mandatory power—in this case, England—which continued in 1920, 1921, 1925, 1929, 1933, 1936 and right up to the end of the Second World War. We were protesting against the establishment of a National Zionist Home on our land. At this time, it was referred to only as a "spiritual refuge" for the Jews who had been persecuted in Europe during the Second World War.

The armed resistance came into being during the Mandate when Great Britain was one of the most powerful empires in the world. When the partition of Palestine was agreed to by the United Nations on November 29, 1947—in line with the official report submitted by the Mandatory power—the Jews were allotted only 10 per cent of the land which they owned.

In the official report, the census for the region gave the Jews 498,000 inhabitants and the Arabs 497,000. These figures were given out on the eve of the partition vote. I question these figures. The Jewish majority of 1,000 was invented to further their cause. These then were the false pretenses on which the State of Israel was founded and which brought it to where it is today: implanted on our land, in our schools, in our cities, on the tombs of our ancestors! It's highway robbery and goes against all morality.

What we are trying to do is to return to our country which we abandoned through intimidation, force and a long list of immoral acts. We Arabs don't like to fight. We are not warriors. We only want to live at peace in our own country.

Our notion of "country" is now under dispute. In December 1967, Ben-Gurion wrote to de Gaulle: "The land of our ancestors has endured many different conquerors . . ." If the Jews are going to use such arguments to justify their actions, the map of the whole world should be revised and corrected.

We want the people in the West to understand that we aren't fighting just for the sake of fighting. Our desire is quite natural. This should be obvious to the West.

Today, Israel is a collection of citizens of many different nationalities united under the label of a single religion. Turning them into expatriates and making them leave their countries to move in on us has been in exact accordance with the Nazi allegation that the Jews were to be driven out of Europe because they were an inferior race, which is absolutely and scientifically untrue!

Why should we, who don't even hold with the reasons given for its existence, support this so-called Jewish state whose discrimination and atrocities against the Arabs are only too well known? For example, young Arabs living in Israel aren't allowed to enroll in secondary schools, or to move around the country without special authorization.

Aren't they ashamed of behaving like Fascists?

We are neither racists nor fanatics. Quite the contrary: we are very tolerant, especially toward the Jews. When the Jews were persecuted in Spain, they found asylum in Arab countries. We are against the Zionist movement because it wants to place our patrimony under its domination. Israel is an instrument of American imperialist colonialism which seeks to appropriate our oil.

America isn't a nation at all. It's one enormous gang! A gang like Al Capone's! They have no moral sense. It's a mixture of people of different national origins, just like Israel! An enormous gang, well organized and well armed!

That is why we are determined to continue the struggle to recover our land in spite of all demonstrations of might. We don't hope to convince any Western nations to come to our aid, but we do want them to understand that we are the victims of aggression.

We need the West's sympathy. De Gaulle himself has admitted that they were the aggressors.

They must be liquidated so long as they are an imperialist state. Our refugees must return to their land. But they want no part of a Jewish state. They want no part of that war machine.

The Jews in Israel are free to stay if they will become citizens. We don't want to annihilate anybody. But we will not accept either partition or the Jewish state, or any separatist movement, and above all we will have no Zionism.

It is only for humanitarian reasons that we allow them to stay. There is no question of recognizing their right to make a nation out of our land. And it goes without saying, they should not be punished for the mistakes of their leaders. Those who want to return to their original country will be free to do so, even if it's some other Arab country.

When did you join the Palestine Liberation Organization?

I joined the P.L.O. at the time of the Israeli aggression in June 1967. But I had become involved in the struggle when I was a student.

The commando struggle, you mean?

No. I took part in demonstrations in my capacity as a lawyer. I studied at the Jerusalem Law School, which was founded by the English as a branch of the University of London. And I did a lot of traveling in Europe. Not in France, because of Algeria . . . I visited the Soviet Union and even Communist China, in 1957.

Actually, I am a replacement for Ahmed Shukairy. At the moment, I am the head of the Executive Committee of the P.L.O. I don't know whether I'll be elected president. He is to be appointed by the national council which is in the process of formation. The one before was dissolved. The national council is made up of one hundred delegates elected by various groups such as El Fatah, etc. Before, it had 400 members appointed rather than elected, who were therefore not really qualified or effective.

I mention El Fatah because it's one of the most important Palestinian movements. El Fatah means: he who shows the way back to his country.

Another very important movement is Al Jabha Al Chaabiya (the Popular Front). It is the military arm of the National Arab Movement, the party led by George Habash, a Christian Arab born in Lydda.

Hammoude became reticent when he was asked to talk about El Fatah. He seemed to have neither the right nor the ability to describe its ways and means.

About El Fatah, I can't say anything. Please don't mention me in connection with El Fatah, whose leaders are in Cairo and Damascus. The P.L.O. is a movement for Palestinian liberation and its goal is to unify all the active organizations. That was the substance of the discussion at our last meetings in Beirut.

What about the new P.L.O. relationship with Jordan?

There was a serious disagreement between us on the subject of the part of Palestine to be incorporated into Jordan, because it was in contradiction with our aim of Palestinian liberation.

We have never claimed sovereignty over any part of Palestine. For the moment, our only objective is its liberation.

The Jordanian government has never officially objected to our being on its territory. Rather, it was the conflicts between the different Arab countries which our organization reflected. That is why we have never had an office in Amman. We are opening one now for the first time. Our headquarters should be in Jerusalem, according to our constitution—the National Charter—but since June '67 our headquarters have been temporarily located in Cairo.

What has become of Shukairy?

Actually, he was asked to leave. I replaced him as acting president.

What do you think of the way he acted toward Jordan and Hussein? Of statements like "We must liberate Amman before we liberate Tel Aviv"?

We didn't approve of either his manner or method. All the same, Shukairy expressed an opinion many of us shared. The same could be said for his attacks against the politics of the Jordanian government, which didn't always correspond to our politics or our goals.

If Palestine were liberated, what would happen to the part that is now integrated with Jordan?

The Palestinian people would have to decide that for themselves. No state or person has the right to decide that for them. Of course, this idea goes against the Jordanian desire for unity between the two banks of the Jordan. Our idea is simply to liberate all of Palestine and let the people decide, even if they want a larger union with Jordan.

In that case, what kind of government would this new nation have?

A monarchy or a republic? Again, that's for the people to decide. We are not against a constitutional system. On the other hand, it depends on the provisions of the constitution. But whichever the case, we want to live under a free system.

As far as Jordan is concerned, we have no wish to be separated. Unity between Palestine and Trans-Jordan is essential. It's basic. At the moment, though our statistics are not dependable, U.N.R.W.A.* figures indicate that the Jordanian population is 75 per cent Palestinian. Only 50 per cent are represented in the Chamber. The Senate members are chosen by the King.

However, there is no use arguing about it now. It is too early.

We are left with no alternative but to fight. And the struggle must be carried on independently of the political interests of the Arab countries.

Imperialism must be liquidated here, in Vietnam, in Latin America, and even in Europe. It is on the verge of realizing Hitler's dream of domination.

I'm an optimist. We will crush imperialism.

In Amman, not everybody shares Yehia Hammoude's opinion. A young Palestinian landowner, Mamdouh Bicharat, says:

The slogan "Arab Nation" is all right, but their methods of bringing it about are bad. In the Arab world, unfortu-

* The United Nations Relief and Works Agency.

nately, we don't act. We react. That's what we're doing now. We don't attack, but we react because they've attacked Shuna and Karameh.

We don't have a definite goal, like "Algérie Française." We don't really know which Palestine we're fighting for: the one before 1947, the one in 1947, or 1948, or 1956, or 1967, or. . . ?

Each of us is fighting for one Palestine or another. Actually, it's for whichever one we'll be able to get!

Chapter 19
The Commandos

"To take Palestine away
from Israel . . ."

During the last week of March 1968, Jordan was suddenly wrenched from its ten months' coma following the bludgeoning of June 1967.

That morning—it was Thursday, the 21st of March—a rumor swept Jordan:

"It's war!"

"They're attacking from the south!"

"They're crossing the Jordan in the north!"

But there was no panic. No sign of excitement. Rather, a kind of relief, yes, as if a pall were lifting.

No resignation. Rather, a morbid joy.

No resentment. Rather, a strange satisfaction: today is the moment of truth. With a smile, they were saying in Amman:

"The Israelis have awakened the dead!"

And on the morning of the Israeli attack, a bus boy at the Hotel Jordan Intercontinental said laughingly to an American guest:

"What's with this Moshe Dayan? At the rate he's going, Washington will be next. Look out, Mr. Johnson!"

Can the Jordanians ever rid themselves of the shame of June 1967?

More than any other Arab, the Jordanian is daily confronted with this problem. Jordan has been at war every day for twenty years. Every Jordanian feels directly involved. You rarely meet a Jordanian who hasn't some member of his family living on the other side of the Jordan in occupied territory. This goes for the Jordanian royal family. For example, the mother-in-law of Prince Mohammed, King Hussein's younger brother, is currently on the west bank of the Jordan. No other Arab country faces this kind of problem.

At dawn that morning, the Israelis struck at three ponts: north of the Dead Sea, at Shuna and Karameh, and in the south, at Ghor Safi.

According to the Jordanian military command, the attack against Ghor Safi was only a diversion.

Perhaps.

It's true that the greater part of the Israeli forces were in the north, at Shuna and Karameh. Tel Aviv claimed that this was only a police action against Palestinian terrorists, particularly those based in the city of Karameh, with its 25,000–30,000 refugees.

Amman snorted.

"Police action! What next! It's a new Zionist thrust. They have decided to occupy certain strategic points while wedging themselves into the north."

Perhaps.

It was even rumored that Israel intended to invade Jordan in the north and south, thus isolating her from her Arab neighbors. No one dared say in so many words that if Amman were driven to the wall, she would have to negotiate.

Perhaps.

Finally, and this was said in whispers, having brought off its gamble, Israel would depose the King and install a provisional government of its own choosing.

Perhaps.

But, it must be admitted, no facts bore out these hypotheses, either to confirm or deny them.

The one obvious fact is the number of men and military equipment the Israelis threw into this "police action," though it is impossible to gauge precisely the forces Israel had available.

It is also useless to try to establish an honest tally sheet for this 21st of March, 1968. Intelligence in this quarter was pure fantasy on both sides.

What did seem certain was the virulence and bitterness of the Jordanian response. Jordan proved that, acting on its own, it was an antagonist to be reckoned with.

This time, there was no question of a United Arab Command, of problematic allied air cover, of aberrated maneuvers dictated by foreign generals. Today, the Jordanian army, which had paid dearly for its confidence in its allies, acted alone and organized itself on this assumption. The program for the defense of the territory that remained assumed the absence of a Jordanian air force, and exploited to the full the feeble resources of the Jordanian land army. And never again would Jordan underestimate the enemy!

Jordanian strategy took into account that its chance of success rested solely in defense. Its tactics were to force the enemy to fight on Jordanian soil and to avoid being tempted to counterattack. This would inevitably place the Jordanian army in a position of inferiority. The Jordanians know that their adversary—leaving aside his superior arsenal—is a master of offensive tactics which are based on his superlative knowledge of the art of movement.

And so, on that March morning, the Jordanian defense was not caught off guard, thanks to a talent rare among Arabs—a sense of positive action, of organization and efficiency. The Israelis were unpleasantly surprised. Obviously, with their infallible intelligence, the Israelis did not expect to be received with flowers. And it is perhaps for this reason that their "police action" was so luxuriously mounted, both in men and matériel: tanks, helicopter-borne troops, and an air force whose know-how it would be foolish to underestimate. And though they know how to take advantage of good luck, the Israeli strategists leave nothing to chance.

But there was one thing the Israeli officers did not take into account: the psychological factor. They failed to anticipate the stubborn intensity of men fighting for their own land, especially when most of it had already been amputated. They misjudged the will-to-resist of people whose homeland is threatened, something which pushes the instinct for self-defense to surprising limits. This will lies deep in his prehistoric instinct and transforms the helpless animal into a redoubtable adversary when any one dares expel him from what he considers his territory.

That is why, at dawn on the 21st of March, the Jordanian tanks and anything else that could be mustered to repel the Israeli invasion, gave back as good as it got.

In Shuna, a little town about 20 kilometers northeast of the Dead Sea, the Israeli Pattons were stopped in their tracks, as were their scouts in armored cars. The Israeli retreat came after bitter fighting. They leveled Shuna and put out of commission a large number of our transports.

On the other hand, the Jordanian defense broke the back of the Israeli advance and disabled heavy tanks and an assortment of vehicles.

It was impossible to add up the extent of the destruction. The information from both sides, as in all conflicts, is undependable. As far as we were concerned, we had visible proof in Shuna of three Patton M. 48's and two armored scout cars out of commission. And on the road from Amman, we came across tractors towing away vehicles we could not identify because of their condition.

The day after the Israeli aggression, King Hussein inspected Shuna. Inside one of the abandoned Israeli tanks was the incinerated corpse of its driver. Two terror-stricken eyes, still astonishingly blue, pierced his blackened face. The King climbed up the side of the tank. An officer indicated the corpse. The King turned his head away and took a breath of this first spring day. The King was surrounded by officers and soldiers. One of the soldiers spat on the corpse of the dead Israeli. To demonstrate his patriotism, probably. The King started. And without raising that curious low voice of his, the King shook his finger at him:

"Don't do that!"

The soldier lowered his head, swallowed and disappeared into the crowd.

The spoils of war were moved to Amman where they were put on public view in Philadelphia Place, the main square in Amman.* For a week, the crowd never tired of looking at and touching the steel cadavers. Some came—a dozen were squeezed into an American jalopy—from neigh-

* Amman was called Philadelphia during its Hellenic period in the 3d century B.C.

boring towns. Just to look. Some came on foot from far away. To look. Everybody wanted to see for himself. With his own eyes. And not only with his eyes but by touching this Israeli metal. A strange need to know for sure that it was so. That this time they had not lost. They had won! The Israeli operation had failed. This time, the methodical invader had not brought it off; he had not taken away what remained of their land. The Israeli defeat was right there, in front of them: immobilized machines, prisoners, witnesses of something new under the sun.

Since then, Jordanians have felt capable of defending themselves and repelling the aggressor, without aid from anyone.

This celebration in Philadelphia Place, open to everybody, day and night, made it possible to wash away the shame of having been beaten so many times. Backs were straightened, jaws firmer.

In Amman, the fear of Israel was being exorcised.

In Philadelphia Place, it was sometimes impossible to see so much as an inch of the dun-colored carcasses through the crowds that shoved to look and comment.

You heard amazing stories in Philadelphia Place: that these Israeli soldiers everybody said were so brave were nothing but cowards!

"How do you know?"

"You know that tank we were just in? Well, the driver we killed was still in his seat. They took him away last night. He burned to death because he couldn't escape. And do you know why?"

"Why?"

"He was chained to his seat! Can you imagine!"

"No!"

"I swear it! And he wasn't the only one. They're so un-sure of their soldiers that they chain them all, to force them to fight!"

That was what they were saying in Amman, the day after the "affair" of March 22. (Of course no Israeli soldier was ever found chained to his post.)

There were also some strange sights on Philadelphia Place. A very poor and blind old man with a swarthy face and long white mustache approached the Israeli tank, tap-ping with his stick. Like a quavering litany, his cracked voice begged for room. Even an old blind man wanted proof of the Arab victory. There was no argument. A space was cleared. The old man was helped toward the enemy Patton. The people watched him in approving si-lence. He stood by the tracks. He spread out both hands—long, emaciated, gnarled, and brown like those of the 25-year-old Israeli driver who burned at his post, chained not with iron but with something much stronger: man's stub-born refusal to break the bonds of violence. The same bonds that yesterday caused a man to spit in the face of another man who happened to be dead.

The blind man's fingers groped toward the tank. A young man guided his wrists. The blind man's hands took it in, saw, felt, caressed, then proof made positive, the hands slowly withdrew from the cadaver of enemy steel, satisfied and convinced. The old man moved away, happy, with only the sound of his stick tapping the macadam. Then the crowd closed around the tank once more and resumed its chatter on Philadelphia Place.

The other target of the Israeli "police action" was Karameh.

Karameh is a camp, a town of Palestinian refugees. Twenty-five to thirty thousand of them. Settled by an act of the United Nations Relief and Works Agency in 1948, Karameh is about 15 kilometers northwest of Shuna.

When the Israeli troops dropped out of their helicopters in Karameh, they met no resistance. The town was deserted. Two or three days earlier, the Jordanians had gotten wind of a probable Israeli attack. As a precaution, they had evacuated the refugees to other camps. The Israelis invaded Karameh, determined to clean it out. Every house was methodically dynamited.

At the same time, Palestinian commando groups made up partly of professionals and partly of men of the town, awaited the propitious moment to intervene. They surprised the Israeli dynamiters as they were finishing their work. Violent hand-to-hand combat broke out.

It was reported by Israeli witnesses that 20 commandos turned one house into a Thermopylae and fought until not a man was left alive.

In another case, they fought until they were immobilized by the number of assailants.

Admittedly, a few raised their arms quite willingly. It appears that one commando struck down his leader so that he could give himself up.

On the other hand, the Israelis say they had to resort to tear gas in order to flush out several groups of commandos besieged in tunnels copied after the Vietcong.

The Israelis also maintain that they took 110 commandos prisoner and seized an important document describing their organization and plans.

However, there is nothing to confirm or deny these reports.

What is certain, because it was there to see, is that 95 per cent of Karameh was blown up by the Israelis. Everywhere, crumbling walls, twisted telegraph poles, skeins of electric cables hung with rags and scraps of household furnishings. The odd, the unidentifiable, the ludicrous were scattered about the ruins. Karameh trembled, staggered and dragged itself in the dust whipped up by the desert wind. There is an obscene banality in the spectacle of any town ravaged by war.

"How many victims do you think there were?"

"Impossible to give an exact figure."

Two hundred wounded, seventy-five dead among the Israelis, according to Jordanian figures. But nothing to prove it.

No figures on Jordanian losses filtered through to Amman. The only visible proof in Amman was when the commandos were buried after the services for the dead Jordanian officers and soldiers.

First observation:

Like it or not, the Jordanian army was helped by the Palestinian commandos. But it's hard to determine who supported whom, particularly in Karameh, which was a refuge essential to the commandos. In Karameh, the army was stationed this side of the town, about five kilometers east of the Jordan. Was it the first to intervene, and was it only subsequently aided by the commandos?

Or, were the commandos the first to counterattack, and were they then assisted by Jordanian artillery and tanks?

In any event, the proximity of the army's defense posts, its prompt response, the noise of the explosions made by the Israeli dynamiters in Karameh, the quantity of equipment used by the aggressor and the difficulties the Israeli expedition had in crossing back over the Jordan to reach its own bases, all call into question the Palestinian commandos' claim that they were virtually alone in bringing off the victory.

And again, at the time of the commandos' funeral in Amman, there were relatively few spoils of war. The endless cortege overflowed into the side streets off the main artery that leads to the Great Mosque. And this multitude which was by turns vociferous, silent or chanting, carried at arms' length exactly 16 wooden caskets. Sixteen. Were these the bodies of only those commandos who had come from Amman, carried according to Islamic funeral rites?

Were the other posthumous victors from other towns and villages?

In any event, these caskets pitching over the heads of the Amman crowds certainly contained commandos. The large number of men in leopard-spotted uniforms, their sub-machine guns slung over their shoulders, seemed to indicate this. And both in Shuna and Karameh, on the day after the 15-hour war, there was not a corpse—Israeli or Jordanian—where the battle had been fought, except for the man in the Patton tank.

To ease our confusion, we were told, as if it were some kind of revelation:

"The Israelis usually take away their dead and wounded after every battle."

As if the Jordanians didn't!

Be that as it may, the streets of Amman swarmed with uniforms and guns of every caliber, all coming from the same direction: the east. The presence of these men who, and this is important, caused not a single incident, was not appreciated by everyone.

The King in particular viewed these competing soldiers with definite suspicion. He was afraid that he'd be over-whelmed—and not for the first time—by these uncontrol-lable men who meant to impose their provocative Arab nationalism on the man on the street.* The King, as al-ways, was faithful to his principle of "never looking for useless trouble with Israel" and was put off by the presence of these hordes. They irritated him and made him worry lest they cause some stupid incident involving Israel. It is important to keep in mind that the questionable activities of Shukairy's bands which plunged Jordan and the Arab world into the war of June '67 were painfully fresh in Hussein's memory. Shukairy was removed in December '67, but his replacement, Yehia Hammoude, had little more sense of reality or reason than his predecessor.

Proof of this is that in February 1968, a mild act of terrorism was immediately answered by a disproportionate Israeli counterattack. Eight hours of bombing by Israeli aircraft and artillery added up to a great many Jordanian dead and wounded, both civilian and military, not to men-

---

* On the subject of this provocative Arab nationalism, a highly placed member of the Jordanian Ministry of Economics, who had been a refugee in Amman since 1956, and was now a nationalized Jordanian, said:

"It's easy to rant and to sabotage all attempts to solve the Palestinian problem when you're in Cairo, or Damascus or Algiers! They forget too quickly that the Hashemite dynasty was the first to shake the foreign yoke off Arab soil. Yes, they forget that it was the Hashemites who relieved the Arabs of Turkish 'protection.'

"Some of our allies have been struck with amnesia, if not bad faith!

"They forget that when the Israelis attacked them in 1948, the Pales-tinians called on none other than the Jordanians for help. And if the Arab Legion had not answered the call, it would now be 20 years since an Arab set foot on Palestinian soil.

"We have no lessons to learn from anybody. Certainly not from some of our Arab brothers, and in particular, nothing where the will-to-protect the integrity of Arab soil is concerned."

tion the damage to Jordanian installations and refugee camps.

To be precise, the Israelis took advantage of this pretended "warning action" to destroy two important radar bases in Karak. They had been constructed by technicians in the U.A.R.'s air force. Thus the Israelis were able to anticipate the coming of Egyptian squadrons of Mig 21's.

The threat of further brutality on the part of Tel Aviv constrained King Hussein once again to put the brakes on the commandos' activities on Jordanian soil. Up to February 1968, Hussein had given them freer rein in order to avoid a reaction just as dangerous as potential Israeli reprisals—that of the Palestinian extremists and certain "hawkish" young Jordanian officers. These men were for the most part stationed along the armistice line, and covered the retreat of commandos tracked back by Israeli patrols as they tried to reach the eastern bank of the Jordan, once their mission on the west bank had been accomplished.

Also, to avoid further incidents of this kind, King Hussein took the risk of disavowing in the name of the State the activities of Palestinian commandos operating out of Jordanian territory. Especially since these commandos had infiltrated into Jordan after being slyly shown the door by the Syrians and Egyptians.

In Syria, for example, the government had put a stop to all commando activity inside its borders. In particular, the Syrians distrusted El Fatah, whose members they discreetly forced back into Jordan, pretending it was for the sake of "the cause."

On the subject of "the cause," Hussein went so far as to

say that he had no need of lessons in patriotism or nationalism:

"If there is anybody who thinks he is a better Arab nationalist than I, let him demonstrate it in his own country and not by using Jordan as his proving ground."

Simultaneously, the Jordanian Minister of the Interior announced the discovery of a large cache of clandestine arms: machine guns, various explosives, antipersonnel mines, antitank mines, etc.

The hour was at hand for the test of strength between the King and the Palestinian commandos.

The Jordanian security forces arrived at Karameh intending to bring the commandos to their senses. The commandos welcomed the troops with loud-speakers braying:

"We warn you: If you move against us, we'll open fire without further notice!"

The security forces hesitated, then withdrew. The Jordanian police had no intention of drawing a brother's blood. Besides, these brothers were not only in Karameh but all over the country. It could escalate into civil war. Government circles were already convinced of it. The Palestinian commandos, buttressed by orders from their leaders in Damascus, were determined to resist any move by the Hashemite army to dismantle their network or to disarm them.

As a result of the confrontation between government forces and the commandos, a schism split the cabinet. The pro-commandos opposed all restrictions on their activities, notably the Prime Minister, Bahjat al-Talhouny, who had played the Nasser game after the Es Samu affair in order to supplant his long-time opponent, Wasfi al Tall, the

President of the Council and a quasi-isolationist. Bahjat al-Talhouny strongly disavowed the actions of his Minister of the Interior. For its part, Parliament met in secret to try to resolve the conflict which seemed to threaten the regime. Jordan saw itself plunging into a profound malaise, but in the end, King Hussein managed to reduce the tensions that gripped his country.

Beyond Jordan's borders, in Tel Aviv, General Moshe Dayan among others decided he would no longer tolerate the harassment of the Palestinian commandos who had victimized so many people in the occupied territory. In effect, Israel was contesting the idea of an "inevitable resistance" as an aftermath of the Arab defeat of June '67. In the Israeli view, the Arabs had lost the war and could not undo this undeniable fact. On the other hand, if the Arabs would not accept their defeat and intended to pursue hostilities by other means, then Israel would not leave it there, but would go the limit.

As if to answer the Israeli argument, a renewed outbreak of Arab resistance in occupied territory occurred on Monday, March 18, 1968, and provoked strong feelings in Israel.

That afternoon, between Timna and Ber Ora, 10 kilometers north of Elath, a bus transporting Israeli school children hit a mine planted by commandos. Two teachers were killed and 38 children wounded, eight of them seriously. It was the first of three buses bringing children back to Tel Aviv from an outing.

The commandos deplored the incident too. In Amman, one of their spokesmen said:

"It was not what we intended. Obviously, the school bus was not our objective. In the military zone between Elath

and Aqaba, our men have planted more than 200 mines—
Chinese mini-mines that resemble little flat discs. The
Israeli buses had received permission to pass beyond the
safe limits so that the children could walk about in the sand
and look over at 'the other side.' As it penetrated the
zone normally forbidden to civilians, the bus was blown
up by a mine meant for military convoys. It's monstrous to
attack children! Besides, the Israelis have the same respect
for children's lives that we do. For example, during the
June war, some Israeli tanks had just entered Jenin, my
home town. Suddenly they came upon a group of kids
around 14 to 16 years old, one of whom was a cousin of
mine. The kids were threatening the Israelis with guns.
Instead of shooting at them, one of the tank commanders
started to give them hell in Arabic. (You know, lots of
Israelis speak our language perfectly.) He said:

" 'You little idiots, give me those guns and go home
at once!'

"The soldiers confiscated their guns without so much as
touching the children, and sent them home.

"I repeat, to attack children is monstrous. This affair of
the bus was a mistake, a horrible piece of bad luck."

In Amman, King Hussein was talking with a Swedish
journalist when he learned of the accident.

"The voice at the other end of the line was talking
English," the journalist later reported. "The King was
very angry, even indignant when he learned it had involved
children. 'It's ghastly,' he said to his informant. 'Incidents
like this are intolerable. There must be an immediate
investigation. I profoundly regret what has happened!' "

King Hussein hardly had time to take action against
the commandos when, three days later, the Israelis

launched their "police action" of March 21. This started the escalation again, even as it tied the King's hands with his own extremists. After Karameh, all that was left for the King was to risk a public acknowledgement of the commandos. During a press conference on March 22, Hussein said:

"The commandos, in Jordan as well as in the occupied territories, give the strictest interpretation to their right to resist the occupying force, just as it was recognized by so many countries during World War II."

He then added: "I assure you that neither I, nor my government, nor our armed forces would agree to accept responsibility for the protection of Israeli occupation forces on the west bank of the Jordan, or in any other occupied territory."

An Anglo-Saxon journalist remarked: "Apparently, the commandos operate outside all control?"

"I try hard to exert control in my capacity as head of the Jordanian state," the King answered. "But it's difficult to tell who is a commando and who isn't. And besides, what do you expect me to do? What should I do to a people who have lost everything, who were driven out of their country? Shoot them? Wipe them out? Besides, I think we have come to the point now where we are all *fedayeen.*" *

This error of the Israelis was psychological as well as strategic. Instead of breaking Arab resistance, it revived it. Thus Nasser, who calls himself first among Arabs when it's advantageous and Egyptian when it isn't, opened up with his hallelujah chorus of " my Arab victory." In Cairo, on that 22nd of March, the warlike atmosphere recalled

* *"Fedayeen"* is the Arab word for commando and means "fighter for liberty."

that of June 5, 1967—eve of the "Six Day War." The Egyptian capital was deafened by military marches and patriotic songs.

In the streets of Amman, euphoria reigned. The heroes of the day—the commandos—made good use of their sudden elevation to stardom to enlist support. They got plenty! Queues formed in front of improvised recruitment offices in every corner of the Jordanian capital.

At the United Nations, Israel's act of aggression was unanimously condemned.

Arabs have a natural tendency toward emotional or visceral reactions, which often carry them to states of naïve optimism. On that March 22, the Arabs dreamt of reclaiming the west bank of the Jordan. The time it would take didn't matter. Time doesn't count in the East—Far or Near.

"After all, it took us a century to get rid of the Crusaders," crowed Yehia Hammoude, the new head of the P.L.O.

The Palestinians had had enough of carrying the burden for other Arab countries preoccupied with their own problems. Jordan was conscious of having acted alone and well.

Now, according to the Arab military agreements, Jordan had a right to expect armed help from its allies.

On this subject, here follows the tenor of a conversation with a member of the Ministry of Information, a man of Palestinian origin:

"Did the Arab countries contribute anything today to help you fight the Israelis?"

"Oh, yes!"

"What?"

"Declarations and martial music."

Here in Amman, few declarations, no martial music. On the contrary, there was the disturbing sight everywhere of men in leopard-spotted uniforms with sub-machine guns strapped to their shoulders: the Palestinian commandos.

A disturbing phenomenon, because these Palestinian commandos are dedicated to going to the limit which tends to compromise the frail chance for a dialogue between Arabs and Israelis. And how can you arrive at the "just peace" King Hussein talked about if not by a dialogue?

Moreover, how can you establish this dialogue when one of the participants—and the most likely to negotiate—has lost the major part of his territory, and that, the guerrillas' favorite stamping ground?

That is why, before Jordan took its place at the conference table, Jordan demanded that Israel withdraw to the pre-June 1967 borders.

Within these borders, there is Jerusalem, an enormous fortress crammed with explosive issues.

For Jordan, as for the Arab world, Jerusalem is a deep wound of many layers, one of which exasperates the religious and spiritual sensibilities of Islam. In Jerusalem, Islam has its cult, its temple, its relics, as do the Israelis and the Christians.

The door that could open the way to negotiations of the Palestinian problem has three rusty hinges: Jerusalem, the refugees and the commandos: the commandos, the refugees and Jerusalem.

It's a kind of *leitmotiv:* Jerusalem, refugees, commandos.

Some of the Palestinian commandos regrouped in Karameh, four kilometers from the Jordan. On March 25, we were given an interview with one of their leaders who wished to keep his anonymity. The man referred to may have been Abou Ammar, one of the leaders in Karameh and an Egyptian by birth. He is about 28 years old. In his student days, he was trained in guerrilla warfare in Moscow and Prague. He looked quite different from his comrades. His head was bare, he wore a brown sweater over a tan shirt open at the throat. His pants were the same color as his shirt. On his feet he wore *pataugas* of light colored cotton with very thick rubber soles. He was the first we had seen with an automatic, which he carried in a fake leather holster closed by two rust-proof snaps. He talked in a pedantic but precise English.

The interview took place in the dispensary of the refugee town the Israeli troops had leveled on the 21st. Nothing remained of the dispensary but its roof and walls. Medications and bandages were piled on the cement floor. Two American journalists were asking questions. A half dozen commandos listened, guns in hand. Only the leader answered:

"The fighting in Karameh marked the first time you joined forces with regular Jordanian troops. How much of this do you expect to do?"

"This is only the beginning. What we Palestinians are attempting now is for the benefit of the next generation. We have to do it since none of the major powers nor the United Nations want to find a solution to the Palestinian problem."

"This could take a long time."

"Obviously. We expect a long war. We know this."

"What is it you really want?"

"It's quite simple. We want Palestine. And for us, the question reduces itself even further: *to be or not to be.*"

"Do you think terrorism is the best method?"

"We have no other means at our disposal. And even this isn't much, compared to the Israelis who receive your American aid. Besides, what do you call the destruction of Karameh?"

"What about your activities on the west bank, what is your immediate goal? Is it political?"

"Our goal is human, not political. We must rouse public opinion, jolt the Arab world and wake up its conscience. After each of our operations, there is a reaction in the Arab world. On Thursday, we fought for nearly 15 hours with no air assistance whatever. Those who can must come to our aid if they really want to find a solution. If we must, we will force them."

"Do you think that war is a good way?"

"We want peace. It's the Israelis who ask for war by driving us from our land. Perhaps you forget, but Israel's war against the Arabs did not start yesterday. We want a just solution.* If we must, we'll send five million Arabs to the United States to help Johnson find this solution."

The commando took out a cigarette and looked around for a light. Someone offered him a lighter. He tried to work it. When he finally succeeded, he said, laughing:

"See, this is all the Americans are able to send us! Cigarette lighters that don't work. That's American aid for the Arabs in Palestine! But the Israelis get Mirages."

---

* This point of view explains why the Jordanians, more than any other Middle Eastern state, are determined to find a solution! They want peace. But not just any peace! The Jordanians demand a *just* peace. That is why King Hussein, in his speech before the United Nations on June 26, 1967, said: "I will not speak to you only about peace, for the precondition of peace is justice. When we have achieved justice we will have achieved peace in the Middle East. There has been much talk in these chambers about peace. There has been little talk about justice . . . What Jordan and the Arabs want . . . is peace with justice.

"Mirages are French."

"True. All the same, they are bought with American dollars. As far as I know, the dollar is American money."

"What we want to know is how you are organized, where your training centers are, who supplies you with arms,* how you get them into Jordan, your methods of combat, who pays for your equipment,** everything that might interest our readers."

* Commando arms (Czech, Russian or Chinese) are furnished by the Syrians and the Egyptians by way of Palestinian and Iraqi battalions stationed near the Syrian border. Therefore they escape Jordanian control. When the King denounced the terrorist raids in February 1968, the Jordanians considered trying to cut off the arms traffic by transferring the Iraqi-Palestinian battalions to Jordan, opposite the occupied west bank. But this would have created equally serious incidents with the Israelis, probably leading to a new crisis. So it was decided to abandon this solution.

** The Palestinians in the refugee camps eventually become commandos. They have nothing to lose. Instead of hunger, poverty, unemployment, aimlessness, they find a new *raison d'être*. It is exalting work, not to mention the prestige accorded a commando in Jordan today. Besides they get a monthly stipend of twenty Jordanian pounds (the equivalent of the monthy salary of a worker in Amman), which, whatever your point of view, is better than nothing.

These funds come, in part, from methods of collection first devised by the National Liberation Front in Algeria. There are also private donors. Forty thousand Palestinians work in Kuwait and contribute five per cent of their monthly pay.

Even in Amman, Abdel Hamid Shouman, the millionaire head of the Arab Bank, views the Palestinian commandos very favorably.

Abdel Hamid Shouman is 81. Large and imposing, he bears the scars of the hard life of a self-made man. He is one of the pioneers of modern Jordan. A Palestinian from Beit Hanina (between Ramallah and Jerusalem), he was a stonemason before going to the United States to seek his fortune. He returned to Jerusalem and in 1924 or 1925 founded the Arab Bank—today, one of the most important in the Middle East. Beidas, of the Lebanese Intra Bank, was then merely one of his employees in Jerusalem.

A Moslem fanatic and a puritan, Shouman is a true patriarchal conservative who terrorizes his entourage. He lives with his Egyptian wife (his second), his two sons and the family of the older one. He refuses to allow his second daughter-in-law to live with him because she is a "West-

"Are you sure you haven't forgotten something?"

"So, you don't want to tell us anything?"

"All I can tell you is that we are fighting for our right to live in peace, in our own country, in Palestine."

"You already said that. If I'm asking you to be precise, it's not in order to annoy you but to inform the public."

"The public or Israel?"

"All right. As you wish. Can you at least tell us whether your bases are inside or outside the occupied territories?"

"Inside and outside."

---

erner," so she has to live in Switzerland where her husband joins her when he can. The older son is married to the sister of Shouman's second wife.

For all his fortune, estimated at three and a half million pounds sterling, the old man rents the villa he lives in. It is a handsome house next door to the French Ambassador in Amman.

Shouman gets up every day at 6 o'clock. This is the signal for everybody to get up, with no exceptions. He is the first to arrive at the bank and the last to leave. He tolerates neither alcohol nor tobacco. If he happens to go on a trip, his younger son takes advantage of his absence by inviting in his friends. But there is one rule: everybody must bring his own alcohol and his own glasses. The young Shouman is not about to take any chances with his family's glasses. His father's nose is keener than a gas inspector's! They say that one day in Aqaba, when Hussein was talking to him, he made the King put out the cigarette he had just lit.

Even though the elder Shouman has a passion for walking and for balancing on his hands—preferably in the middle of a busy street—he is a maniac about modesty. One night when he was dining out at a friend's house, the old man had barely arrived when he took his napkin and hung it over a picture showing a girl in deep décolletage holding a glass of champagne.

His older son, Abdel Majid Shouman, is vice-president and general director of the paternal bank and is said to be the Mycenas of the Palestinian commandos. A member of the Council of the Palestine Liberation Organization, he was probably responsible for the ouster of Shukairy.

Another large contributor to the commandos is Farid Saed, a man of 70 although he looks twenty years younger. He is a friend of Abdel Majid Shouman, and is president of the Jordan Tobacco Company, the largest exporter of tobacco in all the Arab countries.

With a weary and exasperated smile, the American journalist said:

"Look, I was in Algeria during that war. The National Liberation Front bases were outside."

"No. The N.L.F. operated from both inside and outside."

"No they didn't. The N.L.F. was based in Tunisia. I know what I'm talking about."

"When you want to liberate a territory occupied by the enemy, you must operate from both inside and outside. This is nothing new and we didn't invent it. Remember de Gaulle! He was in England, and the first resistance movement started there and moved into occupied France."

"A moment ago, you said that in order for your activities to succeed, it was essential to stir up public opinion, and yet you refuse to answer my questions. What do you want me to tell my readers? I have to give them what they expect of me!"

"You have your readers. I have my commandos. And their lives are more important to me than your readers."

"Then what do you want me to do to arouse public opinion?"

"Look around you and tell the truth. A village of 30,000 refugees completely destroyed. What do these Israeli want? To turn us all into refugees? And I'll tell you something. I have no confidence in the Western press, except for a few journalists who describe what they've actually seen. All the others are always prepared to tell the truth when they're here on the spot. But the minute their backs are turned, they tell lies. I know it's not always their fault, for public opinion is conditioned by Zionist propaganda. And we have to admit the Zionists know how to do it! The minute we Arabs fire one shot, the Israelis inflame world opinion. But if they take land that isn't theirs, and massacre and demolish everything in sight, everyone says: Oh, those poor people, they have to defend themselves. We would like front-page publicity too, but not the kind we usually get."

"What have you got against the Jews?"

"Nothing. I have nothing against those Jews who were in Palestine before 1948, like us. We always got along. You know, we have many sympathizers among the Jews who were here before 1948. And it's often thanks to them that we can operate in Israel at all."

"How many sympathetic Jews are there?"

"Well, about 3,000. I don't know exactly." *

"And you're ready to collaborate with them?"

"Of course. Palestine is theirs as much as ours. No, I have nothing against the Jews. In the first place, our religion disapproves of religious discrimination. But the Zionists, they behave like Nazis! Look. Why destroy hospitals and schools? Those are Nazi methods! We will fight until we throw them into the sea!"

"I understand that there are several different commando movements. How many are there, and who are they? ** Did they fight with you on Thursday?"

---

* During the raids on Israel, two jeeps used by the Palestinian commandos were driven by Israelis who had escaped prison where they were serving terms for civil crimes.

** There are probably a dozen organizations for the liberation of Palestine of which four are specifically Palestinian. The most important is El Fatah, the political arm of the military group called El Asifa, meaning "The Tempest." This is the one that worries Israel the most.

According to Israeli sources, El Fatah came into being in 1965. For a long time, it was simply an offshoot of Syrian intelligence. Its first act of sabotage took place two years before the Six Day War. Therefore, its goal

"There is a movement for the liberation of Palestine: it's
the Palestinian people. On Thursday, all the people of
Karameh were armed. And besides, the King himself had
said that all Jordanians were *fedayeen*. We fought side by
side with the army in order to help it, seeing how unequal
Jordan's forces were to Israel's."

"Who do you depend on?" *

"We depend on nobody. We know that we fight alone.
But that gives us complete freedom of action, and it's better that way. For 20 years we depended on the Arabs, and
look where it got us!"

With a movement of his hand, the commando indicated
the walls pock-marked by gunfire.

---

is not the liberation of territory occupied by the Israeli army, but the
destruction of the whole Jewish state. The terrorist organizations grouped
for the sake of simplicity under the general term Fatah include the remains of the Palestine Liberation Army which joined up with the Iraqi
421st tank brigade stationed in Jordan; the commandos of Jattaf, led by
Chafik El Hout, a former Lebanese Fatah; and members of Palestinian
brigades attached to the regular Egyptian army. The Arab governments
whose regular armies were defeated in June 1967 simply decided to carry
on the fight by other means—guerrilla methods—thereby giving the
Syrians an excuse to drag their feet.

* Beside the four new and strictly Palestinian groups, some of Fatah's
members take orders from Egypt, where they were trained. They take the
Nasser line. Others are pro-Baathist and take direction from Syria. But
among these must be counted the dissidents who refuse to obey Syrian
Intelligence's orders.

The commandos who are exclusively Palestinian permit no one in their
ranks but Palestinians and will have nothing to do with anyone other than
Palestinians. Some are royalists, hence pro-Hussein, others are republicans
and therefore anti-Hussein. Still others, the "hawks," are not interested in
political questions and have only one goal: to liberate not only the west
bank, but all of Palestine.

Before June 1967, all commando organizations were dependents of the
Palestine Liberation Army which Egypt had created and placed under
the command of Shukairy, president of the P.L.O.

The gesture drew a murmur of approval from his companions.

"The King granted you Jordanian citizenship."

"Yes, but I'm no more at home in Jordan than the refugees are. To feel at home is not just a matter of official papers, even if these papers give you equal rights with the others. To feel at home is to feel secure."

"And you don't feel secure in Jordan?"

"No more than I would in Moscow or Prague, where I was very well received on several visits. I might even say that I feel more secure on the other bank of the Jordan than I do here, because there I'm at home. It's a physical feeling for the earth where you were born. You may say that to your readers."

"Obviously, yes. But my readers also need facts. That is why I'd like to know if there are many of you *fedayeen* on the west bank?" *

"Enough to do a good day's work. Ask Moshe Dayan!"

"Was it really the *fedayeen* who wounded Moshe Dayan?" **

* There are probably 20,000 commandos in Jordan today, of whom 600 are on the west bank where there were 100 before June 1967. Their number grows from day to day thanks to an accelerated enrollment, for most of them combine their functions as commandos with a civilian occupation. That is how, in Karameh for example, they operate by rotating groups of 50 to 100 men. As a result, El Fatah has cells in every level of Jordanian life. This makes them virtually uncontrollable.

This also explains the higher quality of today's commandos. Most of them are students or young men from the privileged classes. They received an official guerrilla training in bases like Karameh, which was the principal objective of the Israeli "police action" of March 1968. The El Asifa cells are made up of groups of 30 to 40 each, and forbid their members to use their real names. They are given pseudonyms or a number as identification.

** This is a reference to the accident that was said to involve Israel's Defense Minister on March 20th, the eve of the Israeli raid on Shuna and Karameh. The Palestinian commandos assert that it was an assassination

"No, it was the Americans."

"How do you get from one bank to the other? And how do you communicate with the commandos operating on the west bank?"

"Listen: the Israelis would pay me a million for that kind of information. Do you have a million?"

"If you ever get Palestine back, what kind of government do you hope to have?"

"It's too early to say. Before you decide how to organize a state, you have to educate its people. Education is the only valid weapon. And for the moment, while we are educating the people, we have to keep on fighting to get back what was stolen from us."

"What is your ideology?"

"Getting Palestine back from Israel."

"But you are armed by the countries of the East!"

"Whose fault is that? We take our guns where we find them."

"What do you need most beside arms?"

"Your understanding. The whole world's understanding. You need our oil. We need your understanding. We'll exchange our oil for your understanding!"

In Amman, a Jordanian engineer said one night:

"There are moments when I wonder if there is a single Arab—beside the King—who really wants peace. I sometimes think that if peace came, they would kill those responsible for the peace, here as well as on the other side."

---

attempt and that they were fully responsible. They say the Israeli general was wounded in an Arab ambush on the road to Tel Aviv. His jeep was said to have blown up when it struck a mine during a tour of inspection of the units that were to take part in the following day's action against Karameh.

Chapter 20
A Few Remarks

More than a year after the war, or the "so-called" war, has anything happened?

Nothing.

There is still no peace in the Middle East.

On the contrary, thousands of miles away, on another continent, an event of great importance took place whose significance has hardly been measured, and which signals danger to the entire world if the Arab-Israeli conflict is not resolved soon. We refer to the assassination of Robert Kennedy.* Sirhan Sirhan, the Palestinian refugee, with his absurd gesture commemorated the first anniversary of those who died in June 1967.

In the Middle East, there is no longer any point in winning military victories. The peace must be won politically in order that there may be real peace in men's hearts and minds. To achieve this, the Palestinian problem must be resolved before it's too late. This doesn't concern only Palestinians, Arabs and Israelis, but the entire world. During the conflict of June 1967, the two great powers managed not to become involved. But it would have taken very little—a misunderstanding, an error, a provocation or

---

* In November 1966, at the time of the Israeli raid on Es Samu, Edward Kennedy, the youngest member of the clan, was on an information tour of the Middle East. His only moment of bad humor came when an old Palestinian refugee in a camp raised a vindictive finger at him and said: "The Jews killed your brother [John] just as they killed Christ!" Furious, Edward Kennedy answered: "Well, that is an inaccuracy."

a quid pro quo. In the fourth round between Israelis and Arabs, for which the two antagonists are inevitably preparing, would it be that way again? Couldn't a new assassin turn up and put a match to the fuse, as another assassin did in Sarajevo and unleashed World War I?

It's true that neither the Russians nor the Americans are ready to atomize each other for the sake of the Arabs and Israelis, any more than for the Vietnamese. If one supports the Arab countries and the other Israel, it's solely for political and economic reasons. The Middle East holds strategic interest for the super powers as much for its geographic situation as for the resources of its subsoil. They should give proof of this reality: their real interest lies in bringing about an authentic peace which they alone are in a position to guarantee, and which the antagonists—both Arabs and Israelis—want, more or less, to have imposed on them. Left to themselves, Arabs and Israelis will never arrive at an understanding. The leaders of the two camps are at the mercy of public opinion, of their hard-nosed politicians, of their ideological extremists, of their "hawkish" militarists, all of them caught in a vicious circle from which they cannot disengage themselves. Besides, there is no Arab point of view. There are only Arabs with different points of view, as shown in the preceding pages. And finally, in the words of a highly placed Moslem: "No Arab leader is willing to go down in history as having placed his official seal on something he is otherwise perfectly willing to recognize as a fact. Who wants to be another Quisling? And in any event, such a man would never survive the imprudence of giving official confirmation to concessions, even though they already existed in fact."

This explains why King Hussein insists: "The Jarring

mission is our last chance to establish peace with Israel."

First among the problems which the Jarring mission must solve is the question of the Arab refugees, to which another abscess has since been added: Jerusalem. Everything else is secondary and can be readily solved in time. It is not only a matter of "bringing an end to the aftereffects of June 1967 aggression," as the Arab countries would have it, but of getting at the basic problem of the Palestinians.

If the Arabs must accept the reality of Israel's existence once and for all, the Israelis are no less obliged to accept the fact that they will never permanently end their dispute with the Arabs until the problem of the Palestinian refugees is resolved. To ignore this is a serious error. Israel must contribute to the solution of this problem, even though its Foreign Minister, Abba Eban, insists that the problem is not specifically Israeli, but regional and international. To pretend that Israel's contribution could only be marginal is wrong. This is the key to Israel's torment. The Israelis must come to understand that in the eyes of the Arabs—and this includes the most moderate and those most anxious to find a political solution, like Bourguiba *
—the very founding by immigrants of a new state on their

---

* Habib Bourguiba, President of the Tunisian Republic, believes that the Israeli-Arab conflict is essentially between the Israelis and the Palestinian Arabs. "Once this fact is recognized, the role of Syria, Egypt, and Lebanon becomes much less important," Bourguiba said on a recent trip to Canada and the United States.

In an interview printed in the American magazine, *U.S. News & World Report,* he added:

"I consider that the presence of President Nasser does not favor a solution of the Israel case because he is too much a prisoner of his past. From time to time he threatens a new war, or he accepts new proposals. Then he refuses to sit down and negotiate, or he pretends that the existence of Israel has been guaranteed since 1949. He is play-acting a bit."

soil was an act of aggression. They are obligated to offer
reparations. And since this state was created by a decision
of the international community, it too must share the
responsibility.

They say that it will have cost 930 pounds sterling a
head to relocate those who were driven out by the building
of the Aswan Dam. Multiply this figure by the number of
Palestinian refugees—1.5 million—and the total is stag-
gering.

Granted; but it's even more expensive to maintain the
luxury of this Arab refugee "state." You must weigh
armaments and military budgets against the progress of a
region and its peoples, their physical and spiritual suffering, the human lives sacrificed every ten years.

General Bar Lev, the Israeli Chief of Staff, commenting
recently on Arab terrorism and Israeli counterterrorism,
wisely pointed out that these would be brought to an end
only when a solution to the problem of the refugees was
found.

The Israelis will never live in peace, practically or mor-
ally, as long as they have this thorn in their flesh. Winning
a war every 10 years will not rid Israel of the problem nor
make her acceptable to her neighbors. The refugee question must be resolved in a spirit of humanitarianism and
justice.

JUSTICE: the word we heard on the lips of King Hussein as well as the commandos of Karameh.

The Palestinian Arabs are frustrated, bogged down in
misery, and their suffering has led them into the path of
despair—guerrilla warfare—because for 20 years, they have
been treated unjustly.

In trying to establish a national identity, they run the

risk of distorting the issue and forcing it beyond the conflict between Israel and her Arab neighbors who after all—Jordan excepted—are not directly involved in their problem.

It would be far better to irrigate the deserts of the Middle East with desalinated sea water than with the blood of Arabs or Israelis.

The End